MW01141012

The

COURTS OF HEAVEN
AN INTRODUCTION

EMBRACING AN ADDITIONAL
PARADIGM OF PRAYER

by

Dr. Ron M. Horner

The

COURTS OF HEAVEN
AN INTRODUCTION

EMBRACING AN ADDITIONAL
PARADIGM OF PRAYER

by

Dr. Ron M. Horner

LifeSpring Books
PO Box 2167
Albemarle, NC 28002

www.courtsofheavenbook.com

Requests for bulk sales discounts, editorial permissions, or other information should be addressed to:

LifeSpring Books
PO Box 2167
Albemarle, NC 28002
USA
www.lifespringbooks.org

Additional copies available at www.courtsofheavenbook.com

Library of Congress Control Number: 2016920609

ISBN 13 TP: 978-1-365-36786-1

ISBN 13 eBook: 978-1-365-36787-8

Cover Design by Darian Horner Design (www.darianhorner.com)
Image: stock.adobe.com #40278483

First Edition: January 2017

10 9 8 7 6 5 4 3 2 1

Printed in the United States of America

CONTENTS

Acknowledgements

Thanks always go to my family, my wife nearly thirty-five years, my three beautiful daughters, and my sons-in-law, and grandson. Also, thanks go to my friend Dr. Mattie Price with whom we have labored in Stanly County, North Carolina for the last several years and together engaged the Courts of Heaven.

Additionally, I wish to thank my friend, Joel Harrison, a seer with whom I also have worked with in the Courts of Heaven extensively. Of course, Dan and Jackie Hanselman have been of tremendous help in our work with the Courts of Heaven and my thanks go to them. Thanks also to those who assisted me with editing this edition: Karen Welker, Carissa Artiga, and Bethany Collins. Most of all, my thanks to Holy Spirit and the teachers He has brought my way as I explore these realms of understanding.

II

FOREWORD

*W*hen I was approached to write the foreword for Dr. Ron's new book, I was honored and humbled. That should be easy enough I thought to myself. After all, Ron Horner is a close friend of mine and a literal treasure trove of wisdom when it comes to understanding the Word of God.

As I sat to put my fingers to the keyboard, I realized that things might not be so easy after all. Ron Horner is a giant in the Kingdom of God. How can one write a few words? A book about Ron and his contributions to the Lord's work would be easy to pen. But limiting myself to just a few words in a foreword? Daunting to say the least.

My favorite thing about Ron Horner's insights can be summed up in his own words.

"I want a scriptural basis for what I'm teaching, and I want it in context. By pulling scripture out of context, you can develop entire paradigms and belief systems that can lead millions astray."

That's the bullseye that Ron Horner always hits. Truth. Dependability. A level of scriptural accuracy that can't be denied.

If I had a nickel for every time I've read a book that was touted to change my life, I'd have a substantial addition to my bank account. If I had a nickel for every time those books ACTUALLY changed my life, I'd have to borrow money to get a cup of coffee.

The book you are holding in your hands will change your life. If you're wondering why some prayers just seem to go unanswered, and some problems are so hard to solve, the keys to unlocking those mysteries are right in front of you.

Enjoy the revelation and relief that you'll find on the pages within. Thank you, Dr. Ron, for blessing us all!

Joel Harrison
Church in 90 Seconds.com

A Testimony

I really wondered at the beginning of the class whether the Courts of Heaven teaching was authentic. After listening for a while and hearing scriptures being recited and rich descriptions of Heaven described, I asked the Lord for clear discernment. Although the teachers were very confident in the teaching, I was skeptical. I think it is wisdom to clearly discern anything new. After three days of listening and taking notes and hearing remarkable testimonies of people's lives being changed I wanted to experience this new way of entering Heaven and receiving revelation and answers to prayers. My ministry has always been about Freedom, and this seemed to be a great way of bringing it to me and others, but I wanted to experience it first for me personally. Each person in the group was asked to go with two leaders and get prayer for their own lives. We all took turns. Still wondering if this was real, I agreed to a private session. Not telling the leaders anything about my personal life they began to uncover some really painful places in my heart but the one I want to tell is about my son.

To give a background, he had been in trouble at school and with the law. He had rebelled and been so angry, we could not do anything with him but pray. Without telling Ron and others this information he began to see my son and me in a cage in the spirit. He said he was so angry. I began to cry. They didn't know but when my son was seven, his Dad left us while we were out of town. It was such a shock and created such fear and anger in me that my son grabbed those feelings from me during this hard time. Later, my husband was restored into our family, but we were still holding such hurts in our hearts about his choices. This was five years later, and the Lord was answering our prayers to help me with my son. After pulling us out of those cages during that moment everything began to change. While I was healed of great abandonment, it was my son's life that really changed. He started acting different-somewhat repentant-then he walked into our church one Sunday night and gave his life entirely to the Lord. He cried and cried, and the Lord softened his heart so greatly I could hardly recognize him. He and his Dad actually embraced that night and have been getting to know each other ever since. He has been writing music and singing for the first time in his life. His life has been totally transformed, and I know it was fruit from this Courts of Heaven time in prayer. After this experience, I have been a part of many Courts of Heaven sessions for my family as well as friends. Miracles have happened, and significant breakthroughs have come. Ask me, 'Are the Courts of Heaven are real?' Yes-I dare you to test it! It will transform your life and open up your eyes to see Heaven in a new way.

Thanks to all who have labored to teach and bring this new way of prayer to us. May your fruit be grand.

Tracy Murillo, Host
Freedom's Voice

PREFACE

Over the last few years, I have done a significant amount of teaching on "Understanding the Operations of the Courts of Heaven." The responses I have received range from one extreme to the other. Many of the criticisms of the concept of a court system in Heaven appear to come from those who have not read their Bible with an open mind or have only read it with a mindset of protecting their pet belief system.

When I was first instructed to study the "Courts of Heaven," I began by identifying court-related terms that I found in the Bible, such as petition, judge, court(s) and witness, etc. Using my eSword® Bible Software[1] program, I initially found over 1700 verses that in some way dealt with these terms. Of course, not all of them were relevant, but upon further examination, an estimated eighty percent or more would have applied. That is a lot of scripture.

---

[1] e-Sword Bible Software available for free at www.e-sword.net.

After studying the subject for several months, I realized that much more was said about the issue than I first realized and so with some more research, the number of verses grew to over 3500. I know of no subject that has as many potential scripture references addressing the topic in some form. Even if less than half of those scriptures applied, we are still looking at a significant number. Can you name an item that has more scriptures?

We often forget that the first five books of our Old Testament are books of the Law-not merely religious law, but laws impacting the governance of all society. Many nations have modeled their systems of legislation on those found in the Bible. Laws are the guidelines by which court systems operate. We have a book in the Bible known as Judges, chronicling the leadership of the nation of Israel through men and women who governed and judged cases within the country. We have four books that chronicle the kings of Israel who often stood as judges over the nation and even have a record of judgments they pronounced. The book of Job starts out in a courtroom in Heaven. The psalmist David decries his many defenses against his foes throughout the book of Psalms. His imprecatory prayers were cries for justice against those who opposed him. We have Daniel who describes a courtroom scene in Heaven. We also read of Zechariah who, in chapter 3, is found in a Court of Heaven, and Isaiah who is instructed by the Lord to bring forth his case. The list could go on. To say that the concept of the Courts of Heaven cannot be found in the Bible is clearly unfounded.

I have been involved in ministry since I was fourteen. I have attended a Bible college and seminary. I also have two doctoral degrees in ministry and quite a lot of study time under my belt. As a teacher by nature, I want a scriptural basis for what I am teaching, and I want it in context. By pulling scripture out of context, one can entire paradigms and belief systems can be developed that can lead millions astray. If the Courts of Heaven is an important concept that we need to understand, then we will be able to find it in the Word of God.

In studying the Word of God, I realize that many important concepts are seemingly veiled from general view until you begin to explore the idea. That is how parables work. You qualify yourself for the truth hidden in the parable by digging the truth out. Less than thirty miles from my home is the Reed Gold Mine. This was the location of the first significant gold discovery in the United States. In 1799, a young Conrad Reed discovered a shiny yellow rock in a nearby creek one Sunday afternoon weighing seventeen pounds. Not knowing what it was, it served as a doorstop for three years before it was sold for $3.50 to a merchant. John Reed, Conrad's father, begin with family to mine the area for more of the precious metal. In a relatively short time frame, the area became the home for America's first gold rush. It was significant enough that the United States government establish a Mint in nearby Charlotte, North Carolina for the purpose of producing coinage from the gold.

Bill Johnson, the former pastor of Bethel Church in Redding, California, points out that the reason gold is hidden in the ground is that only the diligent will dig it out. We qualify ourselves for the benefits of a particular revelation by digging out the truths of it. The concept of the Courts of Heaven is one such truth.

In the story of the Reed's gold discovery, although the young boy did not have to dig for the gold to discover it, he did not know what he had so it only served as a doorstop. It was not until later that its value began to be understood.

Some have wanted to find a long treatise in the Word that would just "lay it out," but may I remind the reader that some beliefs we hold dear have less scriptural backing than the Courts of Heaven concept possesses. As charismatics we value the idea of the Baptism in the Holy Spirit; however, to come to embrace such a concept requires a snippet of scripture here and a piece in another place. It is not so neatly laid out as we would like. The fact that it is not neatly laid out does not diminish its value or truth; it simply requires a bit of diligence to study it out and embrace it. Many other doctrines are the same way (i.e. the Trinity, healing, and more).

Over the course of this introduction to the concept of the Courts of Heaven, I will only identify and begin laying the foundation for it. As you read, have enough openness of mind to recognize that just because you never saw it in scripture does not mean it was not in scripture. When introduced to something unfamiliar, it is natural that we have our defenses up. However, I ask that as you review this material you consider "What if?" What if it is true? What if it is entirely valid? What if it is a concept that has viability for the times we now live in? Is it possible, that this understanding is just now coming to light because we need more powerful tools in our belt to be able to deal with the situations in which we find ourselves? I believe you will conclude that the concept is real, valid, and quite viable for the times in which we live. It is another tool in our belt.

Many of the things I initially learned were via Robert Henderson's CD series on *Navigating the Court System of Heaven*. I am grateful for Robert's ministry and for being a voice for this message. It is my hope that the concepts I teach will mesh well with his teaching. As that occurs, the body of Christ will gain strength and increase in strategy in this paradigm of prayer.

For the most part, I will be teaching in this book on successfully dismantling accusations that are arrayed against us. We find evidence in the Scriptures of several different courts, each serving a function in the Court System of Heaven. In this book I will be dealing with one I refer to as the Mercy Court which some have termed the "Mobile Court." We are instructed in Hebrews 4:16:

> *Let us, therefore, come boldly to the throne of grace that we may obtain mercy and find grace to help in time of need.*

For instance, my great-grandfather had some hand tools that he used extensively. One was called a brace and bit. It was a hand-powered drill with which to make holes in wood. I have a similar tool now, but it is powered by electricity known as a power drill. They both have the same end result, but the electric drill is far more effective and efficient than the old brace and bit. So it is with prayer. We need tools that are even more effective than the older ones. They are still valid paradigms of prayer, but the courts of Heaven touches on concepts more effectively and efficiently than I've seen in the other prayer models. In over forty years of ministry, I have done a lot of praying. Look at the Courts of Heaven concept as simply another tool in your tool belt. It does not need to replace other devices, but it has its place. Let's get the job done!

Chapter 1:

An Old Paradigm

*I*n 1972 I made a distinct commitment to serve Jesus. From the early 1970s, which witnessed the end of the 'Jesus Movement' until the present day, I have watched many other movements come and go in the Body of Christ. I was pursuing the Lord during the heyday of the charismatic movement, the Word of Faith movement, and the spiritual warfare movement. I witnessed the progression of the contemporary Christian music movement from sing scripture choruses projected on a wall with an overhead projector to the current multi-sensory displays many churches use today.

Early in my walk I can recall very few 'prophets,' and rarely did you hear the term 'apostle.' That was simply not a part of the culture of the church in the 1970s. As revelation unfolded, we saw the eventual embrace of the prophetic office, and the further embrace of the apostolic office within the church.

Within that time Jesus' coming has been predicted and re-predicted numerous times. We actually survived Y2K! Remember that?

I have also watched revivals come and go. The longest lasting ones occurred outside of the United States. I once heard someone say that those who oppose the new move of God were often those who were leaders in the last move. So it seems with any breakthrough revelation that comes forth. We certainly know more today than we did in the 1970s. Those in the 70s knew far more than those in the 1950s...and so it goes.

When it comes to our belief systems concerning prayer, we often fashion sacred cows out of them. We are romping and stomping, yelling at the devil, while God has moved on to the next thing while trying to get us ready for the revelation that will follow the one we are now embracing. He is very patient with us. As the church, we criticize the world for doing the same thing over and over and expecting a different result. However, we forget to look in the mirror and see we are as guilty as they. We pray the same prayer the same way with the same intensity when we may have been praying the wrong prayer or praying the wrong way. If what we are doing is not working, maybe we should revisit what we are doing.

Jesus, in Matthew's gospel, spoke of vain repetitions and being heard for our much speaking. Perhaps God wants us to embrace a new paradigm while we hold tenaciously to an older model. Maybe we should let go and follow God.

Let me ask a few questions:

- Do you have prayers that have not been answered, even after much persistence in prayer?
- Have you experienced frustration over seemingly unanswered prayers?
- Have you ever wanted to give up because of an unanswered prayer?
- Have you done "spiritual warfare" only to suffer backlash or retribution?
- Have you drawn back from "spiritual warfare" due to repercussions?

Maybe you have been exercising the wrong protocol for prayer in the wrong setting.

We MUST understand that...

- The spiritual arena operates on legal principles.
- Our prayers must have a legal basis to be answered.
- Don't ask amiss! (James 4:3[2])

---

[2] James 4:3 You ask and do not receive, because you ask amiss, that you may spend it on your pleasures.

3

- If your prayer is not answered, there must be some legitimate reason why.
- Have you met the legal qualifications?
- Have you wanted God to "bend the rules" to answer your prayer?
- Once every legal reason is dealt with that stops the Lord from answering our prayers, the answers will come!

In this book, I will introduce the paradigm of courtroom prayer. Once you see it, you will discover that much of our 'spiritual warfare' has been done while trying to overthrow something that still has legal grounds to exist. We must defeat legally. We often forget that sin exists because a failure of believers to properly exhibit the Kingdom of God. Because of our failure and the failure of past generations, we have handed the world over to the devil and his kids and ran back to our churches to hide. We are hoping we will get 'raptured' out of here before it gets terrible. This is an unrealistic expectation since we have not fulfilled the command of Jesus to disciple nations[3].

We have to become more effective and efficient at dismantling the structures of darkness. The Courts of Heaven prayer paradigm is the most effective way I have ever come across to accomplishing that goal.

---

[3] Matthew 28:19-20 Go therefore and make disciples of all the nations, baptizing them in the name of the Father and of the Son and of the Holy Spirit, [20]teaching them to observe all things that I have commanded you; and lo, I am with you always, even to the end of the age." Amen.

When we legally remove the enemy's right to impact a person, place, or situation, we will see breakthrough released to that person, place or situation. Sin gives him that right, so let's deal with those sins. When we have not removed the legal grounds, we also open ourselves up to negative repercussions. As we get our lives cleaned up, we must deal with the things we need to be taken care of. As we repent for the iniquity that has gone unchecked in our lives and our cultures, we will see a breakthrough on levels we could have only imagined before.

You will regain your confidence in aggressive intercession. You will realize you don't have to go toe-to-toe with the devil. If you do the battle in the courtroom correctly, you won't have to do it on the battlefield. If we successfully deal with the accusations, judgments, and other actions that have impacted our lives and the lives of everyone on this planet, we will see massive change. This paradigm truly is a 'game-changer.'

You will not have to exhaust yourself in 'warring' against the devil and demons. You won't be nearly as concerned about this principality or that demon because you will know how to shut them down. You will rise victorious through engaging the Courts of Heaven, and all glory will go to the Just Judge of the Universe.

Sometimes we wonder why we haven't gotten the answers to our prayers. A short list of reasons for this come from a sermon I heard Robert Henderson preach a couple of years ago. This summary lists some of the reasons.

Reasons Your Prayers Are Not Answered

Here are some of the reasons we have not experienced answers to our prayers:

A.   Unconfessed sin (including secret sin). We must deal honestly with sin...ours and the sins of others (including our nation);

B.   Impure motives of our heart. James 4:3[4] tells us that we are asking amiss so that we could consume it on our own lusts.

C.   We have issues in our bloodline that need to be dealt with. We will discuss this when working through Isaiah 43:27[5].

D.   Men, you may have sinned against your wife (I Peter 3:7[6]).

E.   We may have wrong beliefs or misalignments (John 8:32[7]).

F.   We have regarded iniquity in our heart (Psalm 66:18[8])

---

[4] James 4:3 You ask and do not receive, because you ask amiss, that you may spend it on your pleasures.

[5] Isaiah 43:27 Your first father sinned, And your mediators have transgressed against Me.

[6] 1 Peter 3:7 Husbands, likewise, dwell with them with understanding, giving honor to the wife, as to the weaker vessel, and as being heirs together of the grace of life, that your prayers may not be hindered.

[7] John 8:32 And you shall know the truth, and the truth shall make you free."

[8] Psalm 66:18 If I regard iniquity in my heart, The Lord will not hear.

G.   We harbor unforgiveness (Matthew 6:14-15[9]).

H.   We have idols in our lives (Psalm 24:4[10]).

I.   Broken covenants (Leviticus 26:14-15)

J.   Innocent bloodshed (Deuteronomy 19:10)

May we deal with the things in our lives that impact our prayer life. Naturally, other reasons may exist for unanswered prayers, but this will give you some food for thought. I will discuss in more details some of the reasons listed above as we continue.

I wish to remind you that this book is not a reflection of the other paradigms of prayer which you will discover as you progress. It simply is an introduction of a new wineskin. One we need to embrace while valuing the old wineskins. Each has its place. Each has value, but why use a handsaw to fell a tree, when you may have a chainsaw available?

In this book, you will learn about this paradigm and how to apply the principles relating to it, but first, let me lay the groundwork for it.

---

[9] Matthew 6:14-15 For if you forgive men their trespasses, your heavenly Father will also forgive you. [15] But if you do not forgive men their trespasses, neither will your Father forgive your trespasses.

[10] Psalm 24:3-4 Who may ascend into the hill of the LORD? Or who may stand in His holy place? [4] He who has clean hands and a pure heart, Who has not lifted up his soul to an idol, Nor sworn deceitfully.

CHAPTER 2:

THREE PARADIGMS OF PRAYER

A paradigm is a model of actions or beliefs. In Luke 11, Jesus begins to teach his disciples about prayer. As Jesus was prone to do, he taught his disciples in stages. Starting in verse 1 we read a very familiar passage of scripture. It is Luke's account of "The Lord's Prayer."

> *Now it came to pass, as He was praying in a certain place, when He ceased, that one of His disciples said to Him, "Lord, teach us to pray, as John also taught his disciples." ² So He said to them, "When you pray, say: Our Father in Heaven, hallowed be Your name. Your kingdom come. Your will be done on earth as it is in Heaven. ³ Give us day by day our daily bread. ⁴ And forgive us our sins, for we also forgive everyone who is indebted to us. And do not lead us into temptation, but deliver us from the evil one." (Luke 11:1-4)*

A cursory Google™ search found no less than 200 books on "The Lord's Prayer." Doubtless, nearly everyone you know has heard of this model prayer Jesus taught his disciples. As we are all familiar with it, and over 200 books have been written that explore this prayer, we will not add to those.

FRIEND-TO-FRIEND PARADIGM

Jesus continues with a passage about which little has been written, and it seems little has been well understood:

> [5] *And He said to them, "Which of you shall have a friend, and go to him at midnight and say to him, 'Friend, lend me three loaves;* [6] *for a friend of mine has come to me on his journey, and I have nothing to set before him';* [7] *and he will answer from within and say, 'Do not trouble me; the door is now shut, and my children are with me in bed; I cannot rise and give to you'?* [8] *I say to you, though he will not rise and give to him because he is his friend, yet because of his persistence he will rise and give him as many as he needs.* [9] *"So I say to you, ask, and it will be given to you; seek, and you will find; knock, and it will be opened to you.* [10] *For everyone who asks receives, and he who seeks finds, and to him who knocks it will be opened. (Luke 11:5-8)*

Jesus introduces a prayer paradigm I refer to as the "Friend-to-Friend" model. Jesus references his disciples asking "Which of you shall have a friend...?" And the story proceeds. A very particular aspect of this kind of prayer is persistence. The friend can ask and keep on asking, seek and keep on seeking, or knock and keep on knocking. These are all permissible behaviors in the protocol of this type of prayer.

SON TO FATHER PARADIGM

Subtly Jesus introduces the next paradigm of prayer as we read beginning in verse 11:

> [11] *If a son asks for bread from any father among you, will he give him a stone? Or if he asks for a fish, will he give him a serpent instead of a fish?* [12] *Or if he asks for an egg, will he offer him a scorpion?* [13] *If you then, being evil, know how to give good gifts to your children, how much more will your heavenly Father give the Holy Spirit to those who ask Him!" (Luke 11:11-13)*

We need to notice that in this paradigm, the son is asking the father. In the previous model, the friend is asking his friend. Jesus goes on to tell of the Heavenly Father's willingness to answer and supply. It is apparent from this verse that he views Holy Spirit as a good gift that the Father wants us all to have. In John 14-16 Jesus details for his disciples the many things Holy Spirit will do as he makes Jesus more real in our lives. Ours is to be a life of cooperation with Holy Spirit. We do not have to contend with God; rather, we get to cooperate with Him.

The 'Son to Father' paradigm is the one on which The Lord's Prayer is built as we are taught to pray, 'Our Father...'. It is the most common paradigm with which we are all familiar. I expect many of the readers of this book were not even aware that other paradigms existed when it comes to the subject of prayer. Multitudes of books have been written on this type of prayer while the third paradigm has remained in relative obscurity until the last few years. Just like John Reed's door stop, it was gold the entire time, not merely when it was identified as gold.

Courtroom Paradigm

At the end of verse 13 in Luke 11, we apparently have a change of scenery as Jesus is now among the multitudes of people and exorcising a demon. Jesus does not resume any teaching on prayer for several chapters before we pick up the next portion of his teaching on prayer. Jesus would often approach a subject, back off and give his disciples time to digest the material and then pick up the topic again. We proceed now to the third paradigm in Luke 18 where clearly he is speaking on the theme of prayer again:

> *[1] Then He spoke a parable to them, that **men always ought to pray** and not lose heart, [2] saying: "There was in a certain city a **judge** who did not fear God nor regard man. [3] Now there was a widow in that city; and she came to him, saying, 'Get justice for me from my adversary.' [4] And he would not for a while; but afterward he said within himself, 'Though I do not fear God nor regard man, [5] yet because this widow troubles me I will avenge her, lest by her continual coming she weary me.' " [6] Then the Lord said, "Hear what the unjust judge said. [7] And shall God not avenge His own elect who cry out day and night to Him, though He bears long with them? [8] I tell you that He will avenge them speedily. Nevertheless,*

when the Son of Man comes, will He really find faith on the earth?" (Luke 18:1-8)

We can see from the context of this passage that:

1. Jesus is speaking about prayer;
2. He has put prayer in a courtroom setting;
3. He has provided a system that will give justice and relief from an adversary.

Shortly, I will discuss some more points from this passage, but let us look at these aspects. First, it is Jesus speaking. If you have a red-letter edition of the Bible, these verses are printed in red. We have to acknowledge that it must be something important because Jesus is saying it and the subject matter is prayer. He gives us a clue that it has to be more closely examined to extract the truths within because he refers to it as a parable.

ANY TIME YOU READ A PARABLE,
UNDERSTAND THAT IT HAS DEEPER TRUTHS
THAN ARE APPARENT ON THE SURFACE.

Secondly, Jesus has put prayer in a courtroom setting. Very simply, where do you find a judge? In a courtroom, of course. It should be clear to us that the judge is overseeing the activity within a courtroom and that this widow has come seeking justice. This passage unmistakably places a prayer paradigm in the context of a courtroom. He is dropping us a hint, but we (as the body of Christ) have been very slow to catch it.

Third, the widow is seeking justice from her adversary. In eastern culture, a widow was not a respected person. In some circles, she was viewed as cursed. She often lost any possessions she may have had with her husband before the start of her widowhood. We do not have any information about how or why she became a widow, but anytime you see a widow in the Bible, things were usually going pretty badly for them.

The judge in this parable did not fear God, nor man indicating he was probably a strong individual--one you did not want to cross. However, the position he held as judge enabled him to make decisions affecting the lives of people who came before him. This widow apparently had been contending with an adversary for some time and felt that injustice was involved. Her cry was simply, "Get justice for me from my adversary!"[11]

We will talk about what an adversary is a bit later. As we go through this passage, the difficulty will be covering all the aspects that need to be covered while keeping the thoughts cohesive. I will be referring back to this passage several times in this book because it contains so much more than we have ever appreciated.

Let's pick up at verse 4:

----

[11] Luke 18:3

⁴ And he (the judge) would not for a while; but afterward, he said within himself, 'Though I do not fear God nor regard man, ⁵ yet because this widow troubles me I will avenge her, lest by her continual coming she weary me.'"

The judge in this story does not share all the characteristics of God, but he does share a few of them.

1. *He did not fear man (v.2).* God, of course, cannot fear himself, however, as Supreme God, he also has no need to fear any other gods as they are all lesser gods to Him. God also has no fear of man, though man generally has some degree of fear of God.

2. *...she (the widow) came to him... (v. 3)* - The judge was approachable. The widow came to him and spoke freely to him. God certainly bears those characteristics as we are instructed in Hebrews 4:16 to come boldly before the throne of grace. He does not carry the characteristics of being brash and brazen as the judge in the parable did, however.

3. *He was responsive to the widow (v. 4-5).* In the parable, he was not initially responsive (unlike God). However, he did respond. The Amplified Version translates v. 5 has an almost humorous take on this verse:

   Yet because this widow continues to bother me, I will defend and protect and avenge her, lest she give me intolerable annoyance and wear me out by her continual coming or at the last she come and rail on me or assault me or strangle me. (Luke 18:5 AMP)

The translators' view of this verse pointed out the *intolerable annoyance'* and how this judge felt the widow would "wear me out by her continual coming." The widow was persistent if nothing else.

Finally, he laments that *'she might come and rail on me or assault me or strangle me.'* These are somewhat ridiculous notions, but it is almost cartoonish. See the judge with the thought bubbles above his head (like you do in the comics), visualizing the little widow beating him and shouting, "I want justice NOW!"

Bible translator James Moffatt looked at it this way:

'...still, as this widow is bothering me, I will see justice done to her — not to have her forever coming and pestering me.' (Luke 18:5 MOFFATT)

He saw her coming over and over until by her persistence, she wore the judge down. Apparently, this widow was known for her tenacity. It would not be difficult to imagine that she was forced to be persistent to get what was due her. We do not like to view ourselves as ever pestering God. However, we do have the right to continually come before him. We all have, at times, gone to the Lord in prayer multiple times over the same issue. We are permitted to come before the judge over and over until we get the relief sought. The widow knew that she had the right to continually come before the judge just as we do.

It seems this widow had been put off before, and despite being dismissed, she continued to return to the judge and likely would have persisted until she obtained justice.

4. The widow understood that justice demanded an answer... (v. 3). In verse 3, we read: Now there was a widow in that city; and she came to him, saying, 'Get justice for me from my adversary' (Luke 18:3). The widow, although disenfranchised by society, understood that a court system did exist and that she could utilize it to obtain justice for her adversary. The judicial system of God is available to everyone, but we have to avail ourselves of that system.

These are just a few of the points that can be gleaned from this parable. As we move forward, we will find Jesus had some interesting things to say about this judge which we are instructed to take note of.

CHAPTER 3:

THE PROBLEM WITH DELAY

One of the challenges with prayer is the aspect of delay. We pray over and over and the desired thing never seems to come. Proverbs 13:12 declares:

'Hope deferred makes the heart sick, but when the desire comes, it is a tree of life.'

Many other scriptures address this dynamic, including Galatians 6:9 where Paul instructs us to not grow weary in doing good (or the right thing), for in due season we will reap if we do not lose heart. We will have the answer eventually.

Jesus realized this was a problem and addressed it in Luke 18. Let us look at verse 1 again:

Then He spoke a parable to them that men always ought to pray and not lose heart...

He recognized that when people pray they have a tendency to lose heart unless they saw the answer come promptly. When

Jesus used the word 'ought' it is the word 'dei'[12] which means to do something to fulfill a legal requirement. Prayer in this manner meets a legal obligation. We need to understand that the spiritual world operates on principles of law. If we understand that when we align with those principles, and fulfill the demands of that legal system, then the answers to our prayers will come. Because we have not recognized this fact, we have often prayed outside of the legal requirements of the legal system God has established.

One of the requirements of prayer is faith, yet we have often prayed outside of faith. We have confused faith with hope and not seen answers to our prayers. Sometimes we have tried to point out all the reasons why God should respond to this particular prayer since the person we are praying for is really good and they have not been naughty all year long, and so they deserve it. After all, it's Christmas and God is like Santa Clause, right? Wrong. At other times we have treated God as if he dispensed things from a heavenly vending machine, and if we put in the right 'coins' in the slot, then the answer had to come. Some have felt that 'If I pray long enough, hard enough, loud enough, then God just HAS to answer my prayer!'

I remember hearing Kenneth Copeland speak of an experience in prayer when he was a young Christian. He had heard the term 'bombard the gates of Heaven,' (as if they are closed and bolted shut) and decided that was what he was going to do. He proceeded to 'bombard the gates of Heaven' with prayer and prayed for quite a while in that mode. When

---

[12] Strong. G1163.

he tired and got quiet, he heard Holy Spirit speak and ask him, 'What are you doing?' His answer, of course, was, 'I'm bombarding the gates of Heaven.' Holy Spirit asked him a second question, 'How big is Heaven?' His reply, 'Well, 1400 miles wide, 1400 miles deep, and 1400 miles high.' Holy Spirit then asks, 'And where is the throne?' Kenneth's response, 'In the center.' Holy Spirit responded: 'So you are at least 700 miles from the throne, right? The door is open, come on in!'

Kenneth noted the foolishness of this concept that is actually quite common in some circles in the Body of Christ. We don't have to 'bombard' Heaven. We are citizens of Heaven; we have a right to go to Heaven right to the throne of God. We don't have to beat God into submission (nor can we) to 'get' God to answer our prayer. He is quite willing to, but prayer, like fasting or giving, has protocols that must be adhered to.

Most of us have experienced frustrations like the ones mentioned. We need to realize this truth:

THE COURTROOM SCENARIO OF PRAYER IS THE ONLY PRAYER PARADIGM THAT GUARANTEES A RAPID RESPONSE FROM OUR HEAVENLY FATHER, THE JUST JUDGE.

Let us look at this in verses 6-8:

Then the Lord said, "Hear what the unjust judge said. [7] And shall God not avenge His own elect who cry out day and night to Him, though He bears long with them? [8] I

*tell you that **He will avenge them speedily.**
Nevertheless, when the Son of Man comes, will He
really find faith on the earth?" (Luke 18:6-8) (Emphasis
mine)*

In contrast, the Friend-to-Friend paradigm speaks of asking
and continuing to ask, seeking and continuing to seek,
knocking and continuing to knock...none of which necessarily
imply a quick response. The Son to Father Paradigm gives no
indication of the time that I am aware of. Only the Courtroom
paradigm promises a quick response.

Let me interject a testimony of a widow:

*We went to the Courts of Heaven on behalf of my
daughter. A situation that had gone unresolved for over
three years was resolved within 24 hours of going to the
courts! Praise the Lord!*

- Patsy

The widow in the parable had likely been bullied and
pressed down by others in the society in which she lived. As a
non-person, she was considered unimportant and was deemed
to have nothing to offer society. Often the belief was held that
she was cursed and therefore was the reason why her husband
died. They may have taken away any property she and her
husband once owned. We do not know, although that scenario
is common in cultures that do not value widows. This did not
change until the early church (just a few years after this
parable was told) began to take responsibility for widows as
evidenced in James 1:27:

Pure and undefiled religion before God and the Father is this: to visit orphans and widows in their trouble, and to keep oneself unspotted from the world.

Paul instructed Timothy to honor those who are widows[13], while in the book of Acts; the concept of deacons was enacted as a means of taking care of them[14]. Christianity was the first religion to value and honor widows, but this was not the case in this parable.

Jesus, in Matthew 23:14[15], Mark 12:40[16], and Luke 20:47[17] rebukes the scribes and Pharisees for devouring widows' houses—of taking advantage of the widows among them. The practice was common among them, and Jesus was not appreciative of it. These scribes and Pharisees would consume the widows' houses and then make long prayers, feeling justified in their actions. Jesus points out that they will receive greater condemnation for their actions which did not reflect

---

[13] 1 Timothy 5:3 Honor widows who are really widows.

[14] Acts 6:1 Now in those days, when the number of the disciples was multiplying, there arose a complaint against the Hebrews by the Hellenists, because their widows were neglected in the daily distribution.

[15] Matthew 23:14 Woe to you, scribes and Pharisees, hypocrites! For you devour widows' houses, and for a pretense make long prayers. Therefore you will receive greater condemnation.

[16] Mark 12:40 ...who devour widows' houses, and for a pretense make long prayers. These will receive greater condemnation.

[17] Luke 20:47 ...who devour widows' houses, and for a pretense make long prayers. These will receive greater condemnation.

the heart of Father God. Of course, according to Jesus, God was not their father—Satan was[18].

Because the woman was not valued as a person, she went to the only place where she had recourse against the adversary (defined as one who opposes), and the judge finally relented due to her determination to pester him until he did give her what she was entitled to.

EVEN THE LOWLIEST AMONG US HAVE RIGHTS, AND IF THEY CANNOT STAND UP FOR THEMSELVES, THEN WE SHOULD STEP UP TO THE PLATE AND ASSIST THEM IN OBTAINING JUSTICE.

So it was in the parable. The widow came before the judge with a simple request - 'Get justice for me from my adversary.' (We will talk more about adversaries in a later chapter.) He was trying to take something that was lawfully hers or trying to keep from her something that was lawfully hers. Her cry was simple—it was for justice.

She was not seeking revenge (which is implied in the translation), but a better rendering might be 'Do me justice

---

[18] John 8:44 ...you are of your father, the devil....

against, or vindicate me from, my adversary."[19] The prophet Isaiah had given explicit instructions to magistrates and those in leadership in Isaiah 1:17:

Learn to do good; seek justice, rebuke the oppressor; defend the fatherless, plead for the widow.

So did the prophet Jeremiah, in Jeremiah 22:3:

Thus says the LORD: "Execute judgment and righteousness, and deliver the plundered out of the hand of the oppressor. Do no wrong and do no violence to the stranger, the fatherless, or the widow, nor shed innocent blood in this place."

Please note that the whole context of these passages concerns courtroom activity.

To no longer be delayed in obtaining justice is always relevant to the oppressed. I have seen in our American court system the delay of justice to those who were disenfranchised. God wants to bring our legal system to the point it is actually a system of justice. Proper courtroom activity on the part of the church can bring this about.

In verse 6, Jesus tells us to pay attention to what the unjust judge has just said. Apparently, Jesus thought it was significant, and it contained a lesson for us. Let us read the passage again:

---

[19] Clarke, Adam. "Commentary on Luke 18:3". "The Adam Clarke Commentary". 1832. Public Domain (Clarke)

Then the Lord said, "Hear what the unjust judge said. [7] And shall God not avenge His own elect who cry out day and night to Him, though He bears long with them? [8] I tell you that He will avenge them speedily. Nevertheless, when the Son of Man comes, will He really find faith on the earth?" (Luke 18:6-8)

Jesus is pointing out that our God will certainly avenge his children. The word 'elect' is also translated as 'chosen ones,' or 'favorites.' He is patient with us and in the next verse tell us, *'He will avenge (vindicate, bring retribution for) them speedily.'* No matter how you look at this verse, it indicates that God will respond quickly in this prayer paradigm.

THE COURTROOM PRAYER PARADIGM IS THE ONLY PRAYER PARADIGM TO GUARANTEE A SPEEDY RESPONSE.

Many people who have engaged the Courts of Heaven testify of similar results. I have witnessed long-standing issues being resolved in a matter of a few hours to less than a week. In some of these cases the prayers had been ongoing for three to four years, and in less than four to five days the issues had been resolved. I have witnessed an overnight turnaround in situations that had lasted many months or even years. My experience is such that when I go into the Courts of Heaven, I go in with the expectation that these issues will be resolved quickly. You can expect the same because we have the promise from verse 8...*he will avenge speedily.*

Chapter 4:

Rightly Dividing the Word

O ne of the principles of biblical interpretation is that a Scripture passage could not mean what it never would have meant to those to who it was written. We have to consider (1) The Context - to who was it written, at what time period, and for what time period; (2) The Content - what does it say—what is the message? What other scriptures say the same thing or used similar phraseology? Finally, consider (3) The Concept - what is being taught in the scriptures you read?

I often use this illustration:

In the Bible we find the passage, *'...and he (Judas) went out and hanged himself...*[20]*'.* In another place we locate the instruction, *'...go and do likewise....*[21]*'* Obviously, these two passages are not meant to go together, but they both can be accessed in scripture. If we were to do an honest appraisal, we

---

[20] Matthew 27:5
[21] Luke 10:37

would be surprised at how many times our pet doctrines are guilty of this 'proof-texting.' *Theopedia* defines proof-texting like this:

> **Proof-texting** *is the method by which a person appeals to a biblical text to prove or justify a theological position without regard for the context of the passage they are citing.[22]*

What we often do not realize is that many scriptures were directed at specific audiences and do not apply directly to us. That is not to say that lessons cannot be learned from these scriptures. To take a scripture that was directly addressed to an individual and try to take it as your possession cannot always be done. In the Gospels, Jesus was often speaking directly to the scribes and Pharisees of his day. Some of the things he said were specific to them and no one else. We are often guilty of hijacking scriptures to fit a particular instance. That is often referred to as 'eisegesis.' *Theopedia* defines it this way:

> **Eisegesis** *is the act imposing meaning onto a text and is often described regarding reading "into" the text rather than "out of" it. Therefore it is the opposite of Exegesis.[23]*

Concerning exegesis, let us refer to *Theopedia* again:

> *Biblical exegesis is a systematic process by which a person arrives at a reasonable and coherent sense of the meaning and message of a biblical passage. Ideally, an*

---

[22] 'Proof-texting.' *Theopedia.* N.p., n.d. Web. 3 Aug. 2016.
[23] 'Eisegesis.' Theopedia. http://www.theopedia.com/eisegesis.

understanding of the original texts (Greek and Hebrew) is required. In the process of exegesis, a passage must be viewed in its historical and grammatical context with its time/purpose of writing taken into account. This is often accommodated by asking:

Who wrote the text, and who is the intended readership?

What is the context of the text, i.e. how does it fit in the author's larger thought process, purpose, or argument in the chapter and book where it resides?

Is the choice of words, wording, or word order significant in this particular passage?

Why was the text written (e.g. to correct, encourage, or explain, etc.)?

When was the text written?[24]

It is distinct from Hermeneutics. *Theopedia* describes it in this manner:

Sometimes the terms exegesis and hermeneutics have been used interchangeably. However, there is a distinction to be made. Bernard Ramm explains the difference as follows:

"Hermeneutics...stands in the same relationship to exegesis that a rule-book stands to a game... The rules are not the game, and the game is meaningless without

[24] 'Exegesis.' Theopedia. http://www.theopedia.com/exegesis.

the rules. Hermeneutics proper is not exegesis, but exegesis is applied hermeneutics."^ [1]^ In this sense, hermeneutics may also be seen as the "method of exegesis."

Why is all of this important? It is important because many believers are guilty of 'reading into' a passage what they want it to say, rather than letting the passage speak to them. The scriptures should 'read us,' not merely be read *by* us. It is our incorrect interpretations of the Word of God that have created many problems within the Body of Christ. We need to follow Paul's advice to Timothy and 'rightly divide (dissect) the word of truth[25].'

Because we have understood Scriptures incorrectly we often get disillusioned with God, the Bible, and even Christianity in general. The responsibility for the disillusionment or misinterpretation of the Word rests with us, not with God.

We have further proof that the parable Jesus presented in Luke 18:1 was putting a paradigm of prayer in a courtroom scenario. When we look at the context of that passage and then find similar passages in Scripture. This is known as 'letting Scripture interpret Scripture.'

Then He spoke a parable to them, that men always ought to pray and not lose heart, ² saying: "There was in a certain city a judge who did not fear God nor regard

---

[25] 2 Timothy 2:15 Be diligent to present yourself approved to God, a worker who does not need to be ashamed, rightly dividing the word of truth.

man. ³ *Now there was a widow in that city; and she came to him, saying, 'Get justice for me from my adversary.' (Luke 18:1-3)*

Where else do we find similar subject matter? We find two particular passages that deal with the very same issue. These passages are cross-referenced in some study Bibles. Let's take a look:

Learn to do good; **seek justice, rebuke the oppressor; defend the fatherless, plead for the widow.** ¹⁸ *"Come now, and let us reason together," says the LORD, "Though your sins are like scarlet, they shall be as white as snow; though they are red like crimson, they shall be as wool.* ¹⁹ *If you are willing and obedient, you shall eat the good of the land... (Isaiah 1:17-19) (Emphasis mine)*

In this passage, Isaiah gives guidelines for judging equitably. The courtroom context is evident as he goes on to recite the LORD's urging to 'reason together.' The picture is of two parties meeting for the purpose of mediating a settlement. The LORD invited the Israelites to meet with him to negotiate an agreement for their sins, telling us that though they are crimson red, they shall be as wool - made white. If we take advantage of that opportunity—if we are willing and obedient— we shall eat the good of the land. That is a remarkable promise.

The prophet Jeremiah had this to say:

Thus says the LORD: "Go down to the house of the king of Judah, and there speak this word, ² *and say, 'Hear the word of the LORD, O king of Judah, you who sit on the throne of David, you and your servants and your people who enter these gates!* [3] *Thus says the LORD: "Execute judgment (justice) and righteousness, and deliver the plundered out of the hand of the oppressor. Do no wrong and do no violence to the stranger, the fatherless, or* **the widow**, *nor shed innocent blood in this place. (Jeremiah 22:1-3) (Emphasis mine)*

These clear instructions to the king were to ensure that justice would be done for the oppressed. They were to do no wrong or violence to the four classes of vulnerable people covered in this passage:

1. The **stranger** - the non-Jews living among the Jews;
2. The **fatherless** (orphans);
3. The **widow**;
4. **Innocent blood** - often this passage is used to refer to babies (born and unborn) and those who cannot defend themselves, but it also relates to those who would be victims of violence.

The context of these passages deals with the judging of people and situations and the commands to execute justice. This is not merely passing sentence on someone, but rather seeing that justice was accomplished.

Additionally, we find reference to instructions to the judge that can be found in Moses' writings:

*"**Then I commanded your judges at that time**, saying, 'Hear the cases between your brethren, and judge righteously between a man and his brother or the*

stranger who is with him. [17] **You shall not show partiality in judgment; you shall hear the small as well as the great; you shall not be afraid in any man's presence,** *for the judgment is God's. The case that is too hard for you, bring to me, and I will hear it.'* *(Deuteronomy 1:16-17) (Emphasis mine)*

In Deuteronomy, the judge was instructed to judge impartially -- to the small as well as the significant. The widow certainly fit the category of 'the small.' Because of this particular commandment to judges, the widow knew that she had a right to be heard and that justice was her right to seek. This command even addressed the demeanor of the judge: 'You shall not be afraid in any man's presence....' The judge in Luke 18 clearly adhered to this instruction as it is noted in verse 4 that he did not 'regard man.' In verse 6 Jesus instructs us to hear what this 'unjust' judge, said. As the judge indicated he would respond to the widow's case, he cannot be considered unfair in that sense. However, since it is noted that he did not 'fear God,' it may be that he is not referred to as 'unjust' regarding his conduct in the courts, but because of his 'unjustified' state before God. The American Standard Version and English Standard Version both refer to him as an 'unrighteous judge' as opposed to an 'unjust judge.'

Each of these referenced passages (Isaiah 1, Jeremiah 2, and Deuteronomy 1) pertains to courts and courtroom activity. Jesus was certainly familiar with these passages and these guidelines. I believe it would be safe to say that he knew precisely that he was introducing a third paradigm of prayer -- that of the Courts of Heaven.

The fact that this lesson in prayer was recorded several chapters after the Luke 11 record may simply have been because Jesus (as he often did) only gave bits of information on a given subject. Then, when the timing was right, he would pick up the topic later having given the disciples time to process what he had previously taught them.

Quite an amount of instruction on prayer was given in Luke 11 including the Model Prayer. The disciples would have needed a bit of time to digest the meat he was feeding them that day. As a result, a short while later Luke records Jesus resuming the subject of prayer.

CHAPTER 5:

WILL HE FIND FAITH ON THE EARTH?

he parable of Luke 18 immediately follows Luke's account of the Olivet Discourse (also found in Matthew 24), in which Jesus is foretelling the destruction of Jerusalem and the various troubles that generation would have to endure. We find Luke 17 ending with the following:

> *³³ Whoever seeks to save his life will lose it, and whoever loses his life will preserve it. ³⁴ I tell you, in that night there will be two men in one bed: the one will be taken, and the other will be left. ³⁵ Two women will be grinding together: the one will be taken, and the other left. ³⁶ Two men will be in the field: the one will be taken, and the other left." ³⁷ And they answered and said to Him, "Where, Lord?" So He said to them, "Wherever the body is, there the eagles will be gathered together." (Luke 17:33-37)*

Jesus was speaking to the generation of disciples that would see these things come to pass. The invasion of Jerusalem by the

Roman army culminated with the destruction of the Temple in A.D. 70. Verse 37 found its fulfillment when the Roman army (with the eagle logo on their shields) surrounded Jerusalem and besieged it for four months before the final invasion in which the Temple was destroyed and Jerusalem burned. During this time, Roman soldiers would indiscriminately kill the citizens of the area just as Jesus spoke in verses 34-36.

[George Peter Holford, in 1805, wrote an account taken primarily from the writings of the Jewish historian Josephus. This work is entitled "The Destruction of Jerusalem: An Absolute and Irresistible Proof of the Divine Origin of Christianity." It is available in paperback and also can be read on the Internet. It will open your eyes to that terrible time in history.]

Verse 33 spoke of those seeking to save their life and ultimately losing it. This verse found its fulfillment as Josephus records that some of the inhabitants of Jerusalem would attempt to escape during the siege. Some of them, while trying to hide what treasure they possessed would swallow their gold, necklaces, and money, thinking it would be safe. Upon capture by the vicious Roman soldiers, the soldiers would slice their stomachs open and take the plunder leaving these Jews to die an agonizing death. Thus, those seeking to save their life ended up losing it. When the Roman commanders finally prohibited this cruel practice, they resorted to simply cutting off the hands of captured escapees. It is in this context that Jesus opens chapter 18:

*Then He spoke a parable to them, that men always ought to pray **and not lose heart**.... (Luke 18:1) (Emphasis mine)*

With predictions of persecution, tribulation, famine, earthquakes, and more, it would be easy to see why the disciples would become discouraged, so we see Jesus concluding the parable saying:

*I tell you that He (God) will avenge them speedily. **Nevertheless, when the Son of Man comes, will He really find faith on the earth?**" (Luke 18:8) (Emphasis mine)*

The disciples were certainly going to need a means of prayer that would provide a swift response. Delays in answers to their prayers were not a suitable option. The disciples living through some of these events would have enough to position them for discouragement. They needed something to elevate their hope. Hence, in this environment, Jesus introduces the courtroom paradigm of prayer.

When prayers are delayed, faith often becomes one of the casualties, so to help infuse faith into the disciples he declares that God will avenge (get justice to) them speedily.

It is this promise that gives hope to us in our day as well. We want (and need) quick answers to prayer. We need justice to come quickly on our behalf, and on behalf of the situations for which we are interceding. As understanding of the Courts of Heaven is unveiled to us, we can engage this paradigm of prayer and bring multitudes to new places of freedom in their lives.

CHAPTER 6:

WE HAVE AN ADVERSARY

I n Amos 3:11, we find an interesting verse. God is talking about His people and has a warning as well as a particular insight He needs to bring to their attention:

> *"Therefore thus says the Lord GOD: 'An adversary shall be all around the land; He shall sap your strength from you, And your palaces shall be plundered."*

We know from Peter's declaration in 1 Peter 5:8 [26] and other places in Scripture that this is speaking of the devil. Amos pointed out three particular things that the children of Israel needed to be aware of:

1. An adversary shall be all around your land
2. He shall sap your strength from you (wear you out!)
3. Your palaces shall be plundered

---

[26] 1 Peter 5:8 Be sober, be vigilant; because your adversary the devil walks about like a roaring lion, seeking whom he may devour.

A progression is indicated in this verse. The adversary was in their midst, and his aim was to sap their strength (via accusations), and then he would be able to successfully plunder their palaces.

The context of this verse even gives greater credence to this as we will see.

> *[1] Hear this word that the LORD has spoken against you, O children of Israel, against the whole family which I brought up from the land of Egypt, saying: [2] "You only have I known of all the families of the earth; therefore I will punish you for all **your iniquities**." [3] Can two walk together, unless they are agreed? [4] Will **a lion** roar in the forest, when he has no prey? Will a young lion cry out of his den, if he has caught nothing? [5] Will **a bird** fall into a snare on the earth, where there is no trap for it? Will a snare spring up from the earth, if it has caught nothing at all? [6] If a trumpet is blown in a city, will not the people be afraid? If there is calamity in a city, will not the LORD have done it? [7] Surely the Lord GOD does nothing, unless He reveals His secret to His servants the prophets. [8] **A lion has roared!** Who will not fear? The Lord GOD has spoken! Who can but prophesy? [9] "Proclaim in the palaces at Ashdod, and in the palaces in the land of Egypt, and say: 'Assemble on the mountains of Samaria; see great tumults in her midst, and the oppressed within her. [10] For they do not know to do right,' Says the LORD, 'Who store up violence and robbery in their palaces.' " [11] Therefore thus says the Lord GOD: "An adversary shall be all around the land; He*

shall sap your strength from you, And your palaces shall be plundered." (Amos 3:1-11) (Emphasis mine)

These highlighted phrases give context to understanding the adversary and how he works. Our iniquities (which can be acts that we have done or those of our ancestors) cause open doors for the enemy to exploit. Amos is gives hints that he is speaking of the adversary by using the figurative lion. In 1 Peter 5:8 the devil is referred to as a lion seeking prey. Amos then uses the analogy of a bird falling into a snare. We are brought to Proverbs 26:2, *'Like a flitting sparrow, like a flying swallow, so a curse without cause shall not alight.'* Curses cannot impact us if no reason exists, but if cause exists, then we will experience the truth of verse 11. An adversary will be about the land, he will sap your strength, then, plunder your palaces.

The process is understandable. The word 'adversary' has its root in legal language.

The term as used here actually refers to a being who exercises a prosecutorial function—one who accuses or indicts another person. (Robert Misst)

The Strong Concordance definition indicates the adversary is 'one who puts you in a tight spot.' Accusations often cause you to be found in a tight spot. They seem to back you into a corner and exert pressure on you.

The adversary is also your 'opponent.' An opponent, to be successful, will look for the weaknesses in others, so as to exploit them.

The widow in Luke 18 only wanted justice from her adversary. One of the main methods this foe uses against us is an accusation. Charges are used as the basis for a court case. If you were arrested for a crime, a charge would have to be made against you which formulated the complaint resulting in your arrest. Accusations do not have to be true. An indictment, by its nature, may or may not be true. All an accuser has to do in a court setting is present an accusation with some evidence to substantiate the claim. It does not even have to be very substantial evidence. It could even be false evidence. Regardless of its truth or falsehood, this evidence is being brought against us for something we have done, are alleged to have done, or possibly have never done. It also could be related to something that was left undone in our lineage that is present in our DNA. God may not hold us guilty, but that does not mean the adversary will not try to use it against us.

In American civil courts, a procedure exists known as a default judgment. One of the ways a default judgment can occur is when the party accused does not come and defend themselves in court. At that point, the judge has to weigh a verdict based on the evidence presented. If the accusing party is present with their evidence (regardless of how strong or weak it is), the judge will be required to rule in their favor. This is because the accused offered no defense in court.

This is often what happens to believers. Because we did not even realize a judicial system exists, we never showed up for court. Therefore the adversary (our accuser) has succeeded in obtaining default judgments against us.

At this point, you might be saying, 'That is not fair!' However, we have to understand that the spiritual world operates on legal principles. It has rules that it must follow, just as the Courts of Heaven have rules to follow. If God did not follow his own standards, how could He then be just?

Our adversary is one who is known to roam to and fro about the earth. He is spoken of as walking to and fro in Job 1:7 and 2:2. 1 Peter 5:8 says he 'walks about.'

While walking about he is collecting information about us that he can use against us. Remember, he is not 'all-knowing.' He looks for evidence to disqualify us from the tasks and purposes God has in mind for us. Zechariah experienced this in Zechariah 3:1-5:

> *Then he showed me Joshua the high priest standing before the Angel of the LORD, and Satan standing at his right hand to oppose him. ² And the LORD said to Satan, "The LORD rebuke you, Satan! The LORD who has chosen Jerusalem rebuke you! Is this not a brand plucked from the fire?" ³ Now Joshua was clothed with filthy garments and was standing before the Angel. ⁴ Then He answered and spoke to those who stood before Him, saying, "Take away the filthy garments from him." And to him, He said, "See, I have removed your iniquity from you, and I will clothe you with rich robes." ⁵ And I said, "Let them put a clean turban on his head." So they put a clean turban on his head, and they put the clothes on him. And the Angel of the LORD stood by.*

Satan felt he had ammunition against Zechariah, the High Priest because his clothing was dirty. The High Priest was required to have clean garments. They were not even allowed to perspire in them. Because his clothes were 'dirty,' he could not fulfill his duty as the High Priest. The Lord intervened and had the angel clothe him in new robes and also put a new turban on his head (lest Satan complain about that). With clean clothes he was once again fully qualified to fulfill his priestly duties.

Jesus pointed out in John 14:30

*I will no longer talk much with you, for the ruler of this world is coming, and **he has nothing in Me.** (Emphasis mine)*

The Amplified Version states it this way:

And he has no claim on Me. [He has nothing in common with Me; there is nothing in Me that belongs to him, and he has no power over Me.]

Jesus had nothing in common with his enemy, therefore nothing that could be brought against him in accusation.

As we press forward, we will begin to deal with the purpose of charges and why they must be addressed.

CHAPTER 7:

THE PURPOSE OF ACCUSATION

o understand the importance of the Mercy Court and how it can be utilized to positively impact our lives, we need to know one of its chief functions. In the Mercy Court, we deal with the dismantling of accusations that are arrayed against us.

An accusation is defined by dictionary.com as:

'a charge of wrongdoing; imputation of guilt or blame.'[27]

That is a legal definition, but when we understand that the end goal of an accusation is to divert you from your purpose, we realize we can no longer ignore these allegations. Left unresolved, they will not simply go away. Rather, they will fester causing more and more grief in our lives and in the lives of those we love. Here is one pastor's story:

---

[27]Dictionary.com (www.dictionary.com/browse/accusation) Accessed 8/26/2016.

As pastor of my church, I was merely ignoring the accusations I was hearing. What I did not realize is that although they may not have been affecting me, they were affecting my church and my congregation. Since learning about the Courts of Heaven, I have begun to deal with the accusations and get them dismantled.

> *Rev. Virgil Harris*
> *Calvary Redemption Center Church,*
> *Spartanburg, SC*

We know that our adversary is Satan. In the New Testament, the word 'Satan' is sometimes translated as 'accuser.' Therefore, it stands to reason that one of the chief functions of the adversary is to accuse.

Remember the story of Peter who when he was told by Jesus that he (Jesus) would die shortly was sharply rebuked by Jesus.

*'But when He **(Jesus)** had turned around and looked at His disciples, He rebuked Peter, saying, "Get behind Me, Satan **(Accuser)**! For you are not mindful of the things of God, but the things of men." (Mark 8:33) (Emphasis mine)*

Was Jesus really calling Peter 'Satan'? No, he wasn't. He was saying, 'Get behind me, you accuser, you want to divert me from my purpose. I must suffer and die. I must fulfill my purpose even if it is not what you envision.'

Jesus identified the accusation and its intent - to divert him from his purpose. He recognized that Peter did not want Jesus to suffer and die. That was not his idea of a Messiah-King.

Jesus, however, would NOT be diverted from his purpose—regardless of who was speaking.

ACCUSATION:

AN IMPLICATION OF WRONG OR INCAPABILITY DESIGNED
TO HINDER THE FULFILLMENT OF YOUR PURPOSES IN GOD

Accusations often come in the 'first person' meaning they are designed to trick you into believing it is your personal thought. For example: 'I can never do anything right!' We embrace that accusation and allow it to sap our strength. If it is allowed to go unchecked in our minds, we will start voicing the accusation saying, 'I can never do anything right.' We may then find things begin to not go right. By embracing the lie, we empower the liar (who is Satan). Philippians 4:13 tell us,

'I can do all things through Christ who strengthens me.'

Paul reminded us in Romans 8:1,

'There is therefore now no condemnation to those who are in Christ Jesus, who do not walk according to the flesh, but according to the Spirit.'

A simple way to remember this is:

The Accuser accuses; while the Comforter comforts.

IF WHAT IT IS SAYING IS CONTRARY TO THE WORD OF GOD, IT IS AN ACCUSATION, AND THEREFORE, IT DID NOT FIND ITS ORIGIN IN HEAVEN!

We must keep in mind that the intent of the adversary in incessantly badgering you with accusations is to wear you out.

ACCUSATIONS MUST BE ANSWERED!

Remember, he will sap your strength, then plunder your palaces.[28] He seeks to divert you from your purpose because he fears you fulfilling your purpose. He attempts to neutralize your impact and effect for the Kingdom of God.

TYPICAL ACCUSATIONS

PEOPLE IN GENERAL

---

[28] Amos 3:11 Therefore, thus says the Lord GOD: "An adversary shall be all around the land; he shall sap your strength from you, and your palaces shall be plundered."

Typical accusations people deal with can be these:

- I'm not worthy.
- I'm stupid.
- I'm selfish.
- I'm unattractive.
- I don't have anything to offer.
- I can't be forgiven.
- I can't do what God is asking.

WIVES

Wives often deal with accusations such as these:

- My husband doesn't love me.
- My husband is an adulterer.
- My husband is an alcoholic.
- My husband is a drug addict.
- My husband is a wife beater.
- My husband is lazy.
- My husband is no good.
- My husband is a workaholic.
- My husband is a terrible father.
- My husband is a cheater.
- My husband is a liar.
- My husband is a terrible son to his parents.
- He's just like his father.
- He's a terrible parent to our children.
- I can't please my husband.
- I can never make him happy.

HUSBANDS

Husbands often deal with these accusations:

- My wife doesn't love me.
- My wife is an adulterer.
- My wife is an alcoholic.
- My wife is a drug addict.
- My wife is abusive.
- My wife is lazy.
- My wife is no good.
- My wife is a workaholic.
- My wife is a terrible mother.
- My wife is a cheater.
- My wife is a liar.
- My wife is a terrible daughter to her parents.
- My wife can never make me happy.

PARENTS

Parents often hear these about their children:

- My son/daughter can't do anything right!
- My son/daughter doesn't love me.
- My son/daughter is an adulterer.
- My son/daughter is an alcoholic.
- My son/daughter is a drug addict.
- My son/daughter is a spouse beater.
- My son/daughter is lazy.
- My son/daughter is no good.

- My son/daughter is a workaholic.
- My son/daughter is a terrible father/mother.
- My son/daughter is a cheater.
- My son/daughter is a liar.
- My son/daughter is stupid.
- My son/daughter is a terrible son/daughter.

CHILDREN

Children, on the other hand, may hear accusations such as these:

- I can't do anything right!
- My father/mother doesn't love me.
- My father/mother is an adulterer.
- My father/mother is an alcoholic.
- My father/mother is a drug addict.
- My father/mother is a spouse beater.
- My father/mother thinks I'm lazy.
- I'm no good.
- I'll never measure up to mom's/dad's expectations
- Life isn't worth living.
- I am a terrible son/daughter.
- I'm a bad student.

SINGLES

Singles, on the other hand, have different accusations they may deal with:

- What's wrong with me?
- Why can't I find a mate?
- I don't deserve a husband/wife.
- I'll never get married.

ABOUT OTHERS

We even make accusations about others that are having impact:

- They are a thief.
- They are an adulterer.
- They are no good.
- They are a worthless bum.
- They are a sinner.
- They are a drunk.
- They are a drug addict.
- They are a greedy person.
- They are a selfish person.
- They are a gossiper.
- They are a liar.
- They are a lazy person.
- They are a racist.
- They are a control freak.
- They are abusive.
- They are a Jezebel.

- They are self-centered.

Now that you've seen some of the accusations people deal with, can you see how embracing any one of these can hinder you from fulfilling your destiny? It is crucial that we learn to identify these accusations and get them dismantled so we can stop their impact upon our lives and the lives of others.

If you, as a parent, were to say in frustration, "My child is simply no good!" Imagine, you are now in a court of law, and the accuser is taking those words (that you spoke out of frustration) and speaking to the court. He may say, "Your honor, even her own parents say that he/she is no good!" We have given him ammunition to use against them in the Courts of Heaven. That very declaration becomes an accusation and is utilized by the adversary to impact the child's destiny. The pattern is the same for all of us.

If you took any of the accusations listed on the prior pages, and asked, 'How will this impact their destiny?' we might find ourselves much more cautious about the words that come forth out of our mouth -- particularly those spoken in frustration. We must learn to guard our lips to avoid saying things we later regret. The words that come out of our mouth cannot be erased.

ACCUSATIONS THAT ARE TAKEN TO HEART ALTER
DESTINIES

Testimony of a Grandson

Following one of your seminars, in our session, we took my grandson who was experiencing a great deal of anger to the Mercy Court. He would explode in anger and throw things. His parents did not know what to do. After dealing with the accusations against him, the anger ceased. He is now the top of his class in school.

-A Thankful Grandmother

Another testimony from the same seminar:

We took my son to the Mercy Court. He had gotten involved with the wrong crowd and was involved in drugs. Part of our petition was that God would separate him from the bad influences. In a very short period of time, one of his drug friends had died tragically, two others were put in prison, and the third had to flee the area because of troubles with other drug dealers. My son showed up at the church one Sunday morning and walked to the front, surrendering his life to God. He is now involved in the church, writing songs, and growing in God. Hallelujah!

-A Grateful Mom

ACCUSATIONS REVEAL STRATEGY

The advantage we have when we have recognized the accusation is the accusation unveils the strategy Satan is using against us. If we can identify the accusation, we have uncovered the strategy. Therefore, learning to recognize an accusation is vital.

Here are some key points about accusations:

- Accusations often hide behind innuendo and subtleties;
- Accusations are thoughts that are not generally edifying;
- Accusations start in the mind as a simple thought which often does not have much emotion associated with it;
- Accusations often come as simply ideas into our minds;
- Accusations give us (or others) an altered perspective of us (or others);
- Accusations can give an altered perspective of things in our lives or even another gospel altogether;
- Accusations may be veiled in flattery;
- Accusations, when embraced, can bear the wrong fruit in our lives;
- Accusations are often a perversion of a promise of God.

As we realize that the accuser plants these thoughts to gain access to our lives, we can gain the upper hand. The accuser wants us to believe that these ideas are ours so that we will follow them. However, we always have the ability to choose.

IF AN ACCUSATION IS BROUGHT AND NO ANSWER WAS
GIVEN TO THE CHARGE, THE ACCUSATION STANDS AS FACT
WHETHER IT IS OR NOT.

The devil is objecting to the will of God by our personal
sins, our motives, or due to unforgiveness in our hearts. Other
factors may come into play, but these are common ones.

Robert Henderson, who often teaches on the Courts of
Heaven, put it this way:

> *Every accusation, whether made by people, heard in
> your mind, or directly by Satan or his forces, is an
> exposure of what Satan is using against you in the
> Courts of Heaven! The enemy will use the accusations of
> men in the Courts of Heaven against you.*[29] *Satan is not
> the only one talking junk about you. Often the words of
> men will reveal the strategy of the enemy against you. If
> you listen to the accusations of others: parents, children,
> friends, pastors, teachers, neighbors, or co-workers; you
> may actually discern the particular tactic at work at the
> present time.*

You may have experienced an onslaught of people accusing
you of something. Sudden attacks are evident revelations of

---

[29] Robert Henderson, Navigating the Court System of Heaven (DVD
Series), www.roberthenderson.org.

the nature of the assault. Determine what is being said, and if it is the same underlying message, then that is the strategy being used against you in the courts.

CHAPTER 8:

DISMANTLING THE ACCUSATIONS

*W*e do not have to live as victims to the charges against us. Jesus gave us a strategy to deal with them. However, the way to deal with them requires something we often do not want to provide -- humility.

STEP 1:
AGREE WITH YOUR ADVERSARY QUICKLY

As we read Matthew 5, you will see what I mean. I will quote the passage in context:

> *²² But I say to you that whoever is angry with his brother without a cause shall be in danger of the judgment. And whoever says to his brother, 'Raca!' shall be in danger of the council. But whoever says, 'You fool!' shall be in danger of hell fire. ²³ Therefore if you bring your gift to the altar, and there remember that your brother has something against you, ²⁴ leave your gift there before the altar, and go your way. First, be reconciled to your*

brother, and then come and offer your gift. ²⁵ **Agree with**
your adversary quickly, while you are on the way with
him, *lest your adversary deliver you to the judge, the*
judge hand you over to the officer, and you be thrown
into prison. ²⁶ *Assuredly, I say to you, you will by no*
means get out of there till you have paid the last penny.
(Matthew 5:22-26) (Emphasis mine)

This passage is speaking within the confines of a court.
Jesus is speaking, and his instruction to us is clear:

Agree with your adversary quickly...

We often want to say, 'NO!' I won't agree because I'm not
guilty. Jesus, in this passage, is not implying guilt or innocence.
That is not even part of the picture. He only said to agree with
the adversary.

Why would you want to do that? Let me give you a few
reasons:

1) **Jesus instructed us to.** That is reason enough.
2) **It stops the argument.** If someone wants to debate with
   you, yet you refuse to discuss in return, it ceases the
   argument. Your opponent is expecting you to rare up
   and start fighting.
3) **It puts you in position for the Lord to fight your**
   battles. Paul reminds us in Romans 12:19 "Beloved, **do**
   not avenge yourselves, but rather give place to wrath;
   for it is written, 'VENGEANCE IS MINE, I WILL REPAY,'
   says the Lord." We are explicitly instructed to not avenge
   ourselves. My guilt or innocence is not in question. Am I

going to be obedient to the Lord and obey his instruction here?

4) **I may not be guilty, but if one of my ancestors was guilty, then it is in my DNA.** I may not be guilty of the actual sin, but I do have a responsibility to deal with the resulting curse. If my repentance on behalf of the particular deed will stop the advancement of that curse to future generations, then I should do so. (Jackie Hanselman deals with this subject extensively in her book, *Silencing the Accuser.* I highly recommend her book.)

5) **It won't matter if I did it or not because I am getting it under the blood of Jesus!** We will discuss this more in a moment, because whether or not I did it will quickly become a moot point.

Other reasons exist, but these are the primary reasons.

Reasons people are not willing to follow this first step generally boil down to one simple thing -- pride. We must ask ourselves, 'Did we really EVER not do the deed in question?' Would we have done it if no one was watching? What have our ancestors done that, although we are not guilty of their sin, we have inherited some of the grief they caused?

Jeremiah spoke very plainly in Jeremiah 17:9 when he said:

'The heart is deceitful above all things, and desperately wicked: who can know it?'

A simple four-step process is what I utilize in getting these accusations dismantled. Let's look at what they are:

1) Agree with the adversary
2) Confess it as sin
3) Repent
4) Apply the blood of Jesus

I'll discuss this in more detail in a few moments, but I want to reiterate that it really doesn't matter if I did it or not. Within a few moments, the issue will be covered in the blood of Jesus so it won't matter.

I've had people try to refute the sin on the basis that they did not commit the particular sin, but Jesus did not say to refute it. He said only, 'agree with the adversary.' The agreement begins the process of dismantling the accusation.

Others try to apply Colossians 2:13-15.

And you, being dead in your trespasses and the uncircumcision of your flesh, He has made alive together with Him, having forgiven you all trespasses, [14] having wiped out the handwriting of requirements that was against us, which was contrary to us. And He has taken it out of the way, having nailed it to the cross. [15] Having disarmed principalities and powers, He made a public spectacle of them, triumphing over them in it.

However, this passage must be taken in its context. We must remember when interpreting the Bible, that Scripture can never mean what it never would have meant to those to whom it was written. We must keep this principle in mind. To do otherwise opens the door for all types of wrong interpretations.

This particular passage is referring to Jesus successfully doing away with the requirements of the old Jewish code concerning sins. Jesus, when he gave his life and through the shedding of his blood on the cross successfully abolished the old covenant requirements. Before the crucifixion, the sins of the people were defined and held against them. It required the blood of bulls, sheep, or other animals to have them blotted out. Jesus, by his death on the cross, blotted them out once and for all. The particular context of this verse deals with the erasure of sins via the blood of Jesus. The book of Hebrews explains in detail this truth. It was not and is not referring to the same accusations referring to the same accusations I have been speaking of. What I refer to are the charges which are everyday things you and I have had to contend with. It does not impact our salvation, but it may be impacting our way of life.

Another passage people want to pull out can be found in Revelation 12:10,

> *¹⁰ Then I heard a loud voice saying in Heaven, "Now salvation, and strength, and the kingdom of our God and the power of His Christ have come,* **for the accuser of our brethren, who accused them before our God day and night, has been cast down.**

However, it is rarely quoted in context, which is as follows:

⁹ So the great dragon was cast out, that serpent of old, called the Devil and Satan, who deceives the whole world; he was cast to the earth, and his angels were cast out with him. ¹⁰ Then I heard a loud voice saying in Heaven, "Now salvation, and strength, and the kingdom of our God and the power of His Christ have come, for the accuser of our brethren, who accused them before our God day and night, has been cast down. ¹¹ And they overcame him by the blood of the Lamb and by the word of their testimony, and they did not love their lives to the death.

Part of the trouble with Revelation is determining if the verse being read is in the past, present, or future. I believe they are primarily past tense. However, many of the truths of the Word may be present fact but not be actualized in our lives. The truth is, Satan is the accuser of the brethren, and I'm one of the brethren. I know I have been accused, and I want it successfully dealt with.

I knew of a young man who, although brilliant, had some holes in his belief system. He believed that if he did not believe a demon could affect him, then it could not. Judging from his life, where he walked away from pursuing God, got involved in drugs and illicit sex, as well as other things, demons may have been affecting him much more than he realized. I do not have to believe that lightning can hurt me for it to happen. Some things don't require our belief for them to be realities.

A third passage that has been used comes from Isaiah 54:17. It is a wonderful promise but is misapplied when dealing with accusations. Let's look at it:

> No weapon formed against you shall prosper, and every tongue which rises against you in judgment you shall condemn. This is the heritage of the servants of the LORD, and their righteousness is from Me," Says the LORD. (Isaiah 54:17)

The key to understanding what we have the right to refute is the phrase 'against you in judgment.' Accusations have not made it to the point of judgment unless you have not shown up for court. If you have not shown up for court, the accuser may have received a default judgment against you. In order to receive a just judgment in your favor, you must be present in court and deal successfully with the accusations using the principles in this book and in my book *Overcoming Verdicts from the Courts of Hell*[30]. I will discuss this further a bit later.

Now, back to the four keys to dismantling accusations:

STEP 1: AGREE WITH THE ADVERSARY

Remember, it is easier to agree and trust God for vindication than to try to vindicate yourself.

We have discussed this fairly thoroughly so let's proceed.

STEP 2: CONFESS IT AS SIN

---

[30] Available at www.overcomingverdicts.com

John, the beloved apostle, wrote in 1 John 1,

⁸ If we say that we have no sin, we deceive ourselves, and the truth is not in us. ⁹ If we confess our sins, He is faithful and just to forgive us our sins and to cleanse us from all unrighteousness. ¹⁰ If we say that we have not sinned, we make Him a liar, and His word is not in us. (1 John 1:8-10)

The word for confess implies that we are to say the same thing that God says about our sin. It is an acknowledgment that the deed was, in fact, a sin before God. And if we had done the deed, it would have been a sin. Many times people are not sorry for their sin, they are merely sorry they got caught in it. In the context of the passage, John is letting us know that to think we never, ever did a thing or never would is a deception. To believe that we have never sinned is to make God out as a liar (v. 10).

Proverbs 28:13 reminds us:

He who covers his sins will not prosper, but whoever confesses and forsakes them will have mercy.

I want mercy. How about you?

Imagine this scenario:

You are driving along when suddenly you notice in your rearview mirror the flashing lights of a highway patrolman or policeman. You glance at the odometer and realize you have been speeding. At that moment, are you praying for justice or mercy? I doubt many of us are praying, 'O please God, let him give me a ticket!'

No, we are praying for mercy.

Now, on to step 3...

STEP 3: REPENT

As believers, we should live in a repentant mode. I heard the late Bible teacher Kenneth E. Hagin gave some very sage advice when he said,

We should be quick to repent, quick to forgive, and quick to obey.

Living a repentant lifestyle helps us stay in tune with Holy Spirit. The word repent simply means:

...to turn back from, to change the mind concerning. It is acknowledgment plus action.

We are familiar with 2 Chronicles 7:14,

*...if My people who are called by My name will humble themselves, and pray and seek My face, and **turn** (repent) from their wicked ways, then I will hear from Heaven, and will forgive their sin and heal their land. (Emphasis mine)*

Isaiah enjoins us to...

⁶ Seek the LORD while He may be found, Call upon Him while He is near. ⁷ Let the wicked forsake his way, And

*the unrighteous man his thoughts; Let him **return** to the LORD, And He will have mercy on him; And to our God, For He will abundantly pardon. (Isaiah 55:6-7) (Emphasis mine)*

While Ezekiel reminds us...

"Therefore I will judge you, O house of Israel, everyone according to his ways," says the Lord GOD. "Repent, and turn from all your transgressions, so that iniquity will not be your ruin. (Ezekiel 18:30)

Again, in a passage familiar to most of us, Isaiah points out...

But in that coming day, no weapon turned against you will succeed. You will silence every voice raised up to accuse you. These benefits are enjoyed by the servants of the LORD; their vindication will come from Me. I, the LORD, have spoken! (Isaiah 54:17 NLT)

I like how the God's Word translation voices it:

*No weapon that has been made to be used against you will succeed. **You will have an answer for anyone who accuses you.** This is the inheritance of the LORD'S servants. Their victory comes from me," declares the LORD. (Isaiah 54:17 GW) (Emphasis mine)*

What is that answer? Repentance!

Several translations have made the assumption that we do the condemning, but since we are not the judge, it is typically the responsibility of the judge in a courtroom to make the determination of justification or condemnation. That is why I see it as allowing the Lord to vindicate and bring justice (which is a courtroom term) and allow him to do his job.

STEP 4: APPLY THE BLOOD

At this stage, we simply ask that the blood of Jesus be applied to the sin and to every ramification of that sin. Why do I state it that way? Because when a sin is committed, it never impacts just one person. Others are always impacted. Take a situation where one of the married partners commits adultery. That adultery affects the offended spouse, and if the other adulterous partner was married, it affects their spouse. It may impact children, business situations, other family members. You may sin alone, but the consequences you share with others. Our sins have created massive ripples as when a stone is thrown into the water.

Because I have applied the blood of Jesus, it dismantles the accusation and the associated arguments that the accuser may have brought against you. Satan understands that the highest answer to the sin problem is the application of the blood of Jesus. Jesus is the perfect sacrifice for our sins. Satan has no argument against that blood. He has no defense against it. We now can step into a new level of freedom from that accusation.

THE PROCESS

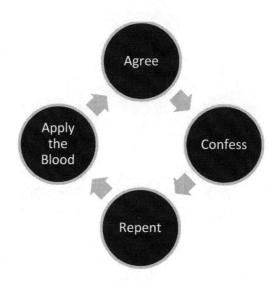

CHAPTER 9:

THE WORD OF OUR TESTIMONY

*E*very person has a scroll outlining the desire of God for their life. Whether those desires are fulfilled or go far from the fulfillment of them is another matter. This scroll is the word of your testimony.

The Psalmist David knew of this:

*⁵ Many, O LORD my God, are Your wonderful works which You have done; and Your thoughts toward us cannot be recounted to You in order; if I would declare and speak of them, they are more than can be numbered. ⁶ Sacrifice and offering You did not desire; My ears You have opened. Burnt offering and sin offering You did not require. ⁷ Then I said, "Behold, I come; **in the scroll of the book it is written of me**. (Psalm 40:5-7) (Emphasis mine)*

And again...

Your eyes saw my substance, being yet unformed. And **in Your book they all were written,** *the days fashioned for me, when as yet there were none of them. (Psalm 139:16)*

Or as the New Living Translation says it,

You saw me before I was born. Every day of my life was recorded in Your book. Every moment was laid out before a single day had passed. (NLT)

We have the record of the Lord's address to Jeremiah,

Before I formed you in the womb I knew you; before you were born I sanctified you; I ordained you a prophet to the nations. (Jeremiah 1:5)

Other scriptures relating to this subject are numerous: Isaiah 65:6; Jeremiah 17:1; 22:30; Malachi 3:16; Psalm 40:8; 87:6; Job 13:26; Daniel 7:10; 12:1. I will not attempt to deal with the subject of predestination or free will which some use this passage for, as this book would then have the length of Leo Tolstoy's *War and Peace* and be hundreds of pages long. You would not want to read it, and I would not want to write it.

Within this scroll, however, I can find listed the desire of God for my life. The adversary would like to keep me from discovering that destiny and thus, fulfilling that plan. He felt that way toward Zechariah who he tried to disqualify as High Priest. He felt similarly toward Peter and sought to sift him as wheat. Others throughout the Bible had similar encounters -- all with the same aim...to divert them from their destiny.

Each of us has a testimony. We live it. We also become witnesses of others, and can then testify of their life. Our scroll, as we live it out, becomes our testimony. We become witnesses to it. Both testimony and witness are court-related terms. In court, witnesses offer testimony of what they have seen, heard first-hand, or experienced.

In Revelation 12:10-11 we have a compelling promise:

> [10] *Then I heard a loud voice saying in Heaven, "Now salvation, and strength, and the kingdom of our God and the power of His Christ have come, for the accuser of our brethren, who accused them before our God day and night, has been cast down.* [11] *And they overcame him by the blood of the Lamb and* **by the word of their testimony***, and they did not love their lives to the death.*

The word testimony means 'evidence given judicially.' What was that testimony? It was what they had witnessed. John, the apostle, wrote in 1 John 1,

> [1] *That which was from the beginning, which we have heard, which we have seen with our eyes, which we have looked upon, and our hands have handled, concerning the Word of life—* [2] *the life was manifested, and we have seen, and bear witness, and declare to you that eternal life which was with the Father and was manifested to us—* [3] *that which we have seen and heard we declare to you, that you also may have fellowship with us; and truly our fellowship is with the Father and with His Son Jesus Christ. (1 John 1:1-3) (Emphasis mine)*

John was giving testimony. In his case, he was doing so to address the heresy of gnosticism that had arisen in the church. Just like John, however, we also testify with our lives and with the words of our mouth. To overcome the adversary, our testimony has to be glorifying to God. If it is not, you can be assured that the enemy will use your 'testimony' against you. If you profess to serve God, but your actions belie that, he will use that in the courts against you. The enemy is seeking to disqualify you from having your prayers answered.

Others are watching your life. Are you living what you profess? Is your lifestyle giving ammunition to the enemy? Or is it speaking on your behalf before God?

READING THE BOOKS

Often it is necessary when going before the Courts of Heaven to request to be able to read the book[31] of the person you are going before the courts on behalf of. To do so, simply go before the Courts of Heaven and ask to see the books relating to the person as they regard to the particular case in question. You will not likely see all their book(s), but rather only what is pertinent to the case. At times, you will see the book or scroll in a vision, or simply hear the reading of the book. At other times an angel will read from the book wherein you will hear the words within you. The words you hear within you which are those written in their book. I have known of

---

[31] The term book(s) or scroll(s) are used interchangeably.

situations where the person, when first allowed to see the book, was unable to read it. The words were in a different language. As they asked for understanding, the words morphed before their eyes, in the vision, and they could then read what was written.

The reason for asking to read the books is so that we will be able to ascertain what the will of God is for that person. If we are not careful, we will interject our will into the situation and our requests will become witchcraft prayers (those prayers that seek to impose the will of another on them outside of God) instead of prayers born of the Spirit of God. We must understand that when going before the courts for someone else, we have to be willing to be detached enough emotionally from them and the situation to cooperate with the procedures of the Courts of Heaven. We need the will of the Father accomplished, not our will. We need what God wants for their lives brought forth.

Just as our Heavenly Father has inscribed His will for our lives in a book, our adversary -- the devil has a will for our lives as well. He has written this information on his counterfeit of the Books of Heaven. Satan is only a copycat. He is not creative.

When you go before the Courts of Heaven, ask that all books concerning you (or whoever you are in court for) be opened. You want anything Satan has planned for the person's life undone. You want what God wants to be enacted. You want their life to match their scroll.

When someone prophesies accurately to you, they have, in essence, read a bit of your scroll and recited it to you. That is why it will ring true in your spirit if it is a valid word. If it is a result of a parking lot prophet or someone just mouthing off something to sound spiritual, disregard it. If it does not register in your spirit as from God, it probably isn't!

When you go before the court you will be asking that all records be purged:

> *I also ask the Courts regarding all accusations made against (the Defendant) by the accuser of the brethren to be stricken/purged from all records (Heaven and Hell, and with all reference to these accusations) that I have petitioned today in the blood of Jesus.*

In so doing, you are seeing the will of Satan being abolished and the will of God being established. Once you know the will of God for this person in this setting, you can be much more effective in the Courts of Heaven seeing the situation handled properly. It also removes your will from the equation. Remember, Jesus taught us to pray "Your Kingdom come, Your will be done!" (Matthew 6:10)

OUR TESTIMONY SPEAKS

The **word of our testimony unveils our purpose in the earth.** It declares before God, "This is what you made me for!" The following testimony is of a young woman who had served God diligently in her youth before coming upon troubling times. Read and discover what God did with her testimony...words she had written as a teenager.

RESTORATION OF A YOUNG WOMAN

A few years ago a young lady I know was going through a very rough time in her life. Her husband had stopped following God, and the marriage broke up. She gave birth to her firstborn son just months before their separation.

At the same time, her church family (with whom she had been heavily involved) basically sided with her estranged husband and abandoned her. Having had a tough time following the birth of her son, she had experienced post-partum depression which complicated matters even further. All this was exacerbated by the lack of enough money to survive on even though she was working multiple jobs. She was in a lonely place. The confusion, fear, anger, and loneliness were taking a toll on her. She was having difficulty making sound decisions and was on the verge of making some bad ones.

A few years had elapsed, and she had remarried a fine young man, but due to the hurts that remained unhealed, they had already separated, just months after their wedding. The son-in-law phoned the girl's parents to let them know what was happening. It was at this point the parents became acutely aware of the situation.

The parents, who lived some distance away, were directed by Holy Spirit to take her to the Courts of Heaven. In preparation, they asked her sisters what accusations they thought others might be saying about her. Words such as: 'You can't do anything right! Why can't you be a better mother? If you had been a better wife your marriage would not have broken up!' These accusations, and many others all piled up to bring her to her present state of being. Her parents also compiled a list of things they had heard others say; things her grandparents had said, her former in-laws, her former husband, her siblings, her former pastor, church 'friends,' and any others they could think of. They also wrote the things they had said concerning her.

They went to the Court of Heaven on her behalf and began a process of forgiving her for the things she had done (John 20:23)[32]. Then they began presenting the list of accusations they had compiled and following scriptural precedent, on her behalf, they agreed with the adversary[33]. They confessed accusations as sin, repented, and asked that the blood of Jesus be applied to each of

---

[32] John 20:23 If you forgive the sins of any, they are forgiven them; if you retain the sins of any, they are retained.

[33] Matthew 5:25-26 Agree with your adversary quickly, while you are on the way with him, lest your adversary deliver you to the judge, the judge hand you over to the officer, and you be thrown into prison. [26] Assuredly, I say to you, you will by no means get out of there till you have paid the last penny.

these allegations and all the ramifications of them. They went through each accusation one by one.

The parents repented on behalf of others who had spoken to or about their daughter, then began repenting for things they had spoken over her life. Some of the things that had been spoken in frustration concerning her, the enemy was using to bind their daughter in various ways. [Imagine, if you will, the adversary standing as an attorney in the Courts of Heaven declaring, "It must be true! Even her parents say that about her! It MUST be true!"]

This whole process took a couple of hours. The parents, however, did not feel as though they were finished. They asked for a court recess to have time to gather some more information on behalf of their daughter. They spent the next few days gathering more information and compiling additional accusations.

A few evenings later, they returned to the Courts of Heaven for their daughter. They presented the other allegations they had uncovered and following the same procedure as before. (a) They agreed with the adversary; (b) confessed it as sin; (c) repented of the sin; (d) asked the blood of Jesus to be applied to the accusations and the ramifications of them.

Next, they presented the promises the Lord had made to the parents as testimony on behalf of their daughter. They quoted (Isaiah 54:13), 'All your children shall be taught of the LORD, and great shall be the peace of your *children.' Concerning her, 'For I know the thoughts that I think toward you, says the LORD, thoughts of peace and not of evil, to give you a future and hope' (Jeremiah 29:11). They presented these and many more Scripture promises on her behalf. Then they offered prophetic words that had been spoken over her life that agreed with the Word of God. Finally, they gave testimony in her own words they had found in a composition book, when as a teenager, she had served God passionately. In this journaling, she declared her heart for God and how she planned to follow him all of her days.*

Once they completed these steps, they asked the Lord to restore her mind, and begin the process of restoration in her life.

Four or five days later, they received a phone call from their son-in-law. The young man and their daughter had gotten back together, she had quit the job that was so detrimental to her, she had enrolled in college, and as a family were on the way to enjoy a family vacation. The son-in-law, said, 'I don't know what happened, but she's back!' The parents naturally rejoiced with them, knowing that their experience in the courts had produced this fruit in rapid fashion. This young woman was released from the bondage of these accusations and was now free to begin making sound decisions, which she apparently had started to do.

We often do not realize that the words that we speak create bondage over people's lives. We will discuss this more in the next chapter.

CHAPTER 10:

THE POWER OF OUR WORDS

*W*e often do not realize how many words we speak that are not life-giving. This passage tells us that we will give an account of EVERY idle (non-productive, unemployable) word. When will this occur? Let's look at this passage:

> *⁣³⁶ But I say to you that for every **idle word** men may speak, they will give an account of it **in the day of judgment**. ³⁷ For by your words you will **be justified**, and by your words, you will **be condemned**." (Matthew 12:36-37)*

The day of judgement that I present to you in not merely a future day, but also anytime when, in the Courts of Heaven, cases are being brought. Due to the words we have spoken, we often have created our own problems.

In Proverbs, we find the Scripture,

Death and life are in the power of the tongue, and they that love it will have its fruit. (Proverbs 18:21)

The 'it' is not defined and could be referring to death, or life. Whichever we love, we will feed. We can speak death, or we can choose to speak words that are life-giving, and life-producing.

Robert Henderson pointed out this fact in his teaching on the Courts of Heaven:

When we are in the throes of trials and temptations we need verdicts rendered on our behalf, so in the middle of all those trials we have to guard our mouths because, if what releases from our mouth is testimony. The enemy takes that before the throne of God, and he applies it as evidence against us and instead of our situation getting better, it gets worse, or it never ends, or it never changes, or we never see restoration from it!

We want to see things change, so we need to learn to guard our mouths more efficiently.

We are instructed by Paul:

Let no corrupt word proceed out of your mouth, but what is good for necessary edification, that it may impart grace to the hearers. (Ephesians 4:29)

Regardless of the party about whom we are speaking, we must be cautious about what we say. We need not give ammunition to the enemy to use in the Courts. This is particularly true if you are in authority over someone's life.

The Psalmist wrote:

'I will guard my ways, lest I sin with my tongue; I will restrain my mouth with a muzzle, while the wicked are before me.' (Psalm 39:1)

Much like you would put a muzzle on a dog to inhibit its ability to harm someone, so we need to do to ourselves.

James gave us this instruction:

Do not grumble (or grudge) against one another, brethren, lest you be condemned. Behold, the Judge, is standing at the door! (James 5:9) (Emphasis mine)

Do not grumble, do not judge!

When we judge someone, it binds them up. It puts things around them so they can't be who they are supposed to be. The courts are rendering verdicts based on our testimony whether it is for them, or against them.

If we say to a child, "You are stupid!", it is as if we have encapsulated that child in a cocoon that demands that they be stupid, act stupidly, or say stupid things. We have built the box they have to live in. The enemy makes a case against them using what we have said. We need to repent of speaking those things to the child and ask that any unrighteous verdict against them be overturned. (I cover this subject in my book,

"Overcoming Verdicts from the Courts of Hell"[34] (www.overcomingverdicts.com).

It is so important that we are careful what we say. Whether we like it or not, our words have creative power. We create futures by the words of our mouth. I quoted Proverbs 18:21, now let us review the previous verse:

A man's stomach shall be satisfied from the fruit of his mouth; from the produce of his lips, he shall be filled. (Proverbs 18:20)

Are we satisfied? What fruit are we producing? Not only in our lives but in the lives of our spouse, our children, our friends, our spiritual leaders? What about the leaders of our government? Are we speaking life or death? David prayed that the words of his mouth would be acceptable in the sight of the Lord[35]. May our words be acceptable as well.

Another aspect of our testimony in the courts involves knowing what God has provided for us through the blood of Jesus. It is our opportunity to acknowledge what we have in

---

[34] Available at www.overcomingverdicts.com in paperback, Kindle, or eBook edition. LifeSpring Publishing (2016).

[35] Psalm 19:14 Let the words of my mouth and the meditation of my heart Be acceptable in Your sight, O LORD, my strength and my Redeemer.

Christ[36]. We have to know our rights and be willing to affirm them in the Courts.

We have a right to access the Courts of Heaven for the following reasons:

1. I am a citizen of Heaven (Philippians 3:20) [37]
2. I am an ambassador of Heaven to the earth (2 Corinthians 5:20) [38]
3. I am a minister of reconciliation (2 Corinthians 5:18-19)[39]
4. I am a son/daughter of God to whom Jesus has given authority over all the power of the enemy (John 1:12 [40]; Romans 9:26 [41]; Luke 10:19 [42])

---

[36] Philemon 1:6 ...that the sharing of your faith may become effective by the acknowledgment of every good thing which is in you in Christ Jesus.

[37] Philippians 3:20 For our citizenship is in Heaven, from which we also eagerly wait for the Savior, the Lord Jesus Christ....

[38] 2 Corinthians 5:20 Now then, we are ambassadors for Christ, as though God were pleading through us: we implore you on Christ's behalf, be reconciled to God.

[39] 2 Corinthians 5:18-19 Now all things are of God, who has reconciled us to Himself through Jesus Christ, and has given us the ministry of reconciliation, [19]that is, that God was in Christ reconciling the world to Himself, not imputing their trespasses to them, and has committed to us the word of reconciliation.

[40] John 1:12 But as many as received Him, to them He gave the right to become children of God, to those who believe in His name....

[41] Romans 9:26 "And it shall come to pass in the place where it was said to them, 'You are not my people,' there they shall be called sons of the Living God."

[42] Romans 9:26 "And it shall come to pass in the place where it was said to them, 'You are not my people,' there they shall be called sons of the Living God."

5. I come as a witness in the *edah* (the church) in Heaven and on earth (Matthew 16:19) [43] [44]

We must know these things and be willing to present them as testimony in the Courts of Heaven.

The words we speak must be life-giving. The fruit they produce must yield the fruit of righteousness. If we are not speaking life, we are talking death. No in-between exists. Parents have a particular responsibility to speak life into their children. As employers, we need to speak life to our employees, vendors, customers, our business...and to all we meet. If we are spiritual leaders, we must certainly speak life to those in our care. In every way—speak life!

---

[43] Matthew 16:19 And I will give you the keys of the kingdom of Heaven, and whatever you bind on earth will be bound in Heaven, and whatever you loose on earth will be loosed in Heaven.
[44] Taken from "Overcoming Verdicts from the Courts of Hell" by Dr. Ron Horner (p. 102) Used by Permission.

CHAPTER 11:

DEALING WITH THE PAST

*O*n Isaiah 43 we find an indictment against Israel where the Lord calls out certain issues He had with the nation of Israel. They had stopped calling upon the LORD and grown weary. Whenever we stop pursuing God, our spiritual strength will lessen. The Israelites had the laws that they were supposed to uphold diligently and had gotten lax. We read:

> *"But you have **not called upon Me**, O Jacob; and **you have been weary of Me**, O Israel. ²³ You have not brought Me the sheep for **your burnt offerings**, nor have you honored Me with **your sacrifices**. I have not caused you to serve with **grain offerings**, nor wearied you **with incense**. ²⁴ You have bought Me **no sweet cane with money**, nor have you satisfied Me with **the fat of your sacrifices**, <u>but</u> you have **burdened Me with your sins**, you have **wearied Me with your iniquities**. ²⁵ "I, even I, am He who **blots out your transgressions** for My own sake; and I will **not remember your sins**. ²⁶ Put Me in*

*remembrance; let us **contend** together; **state your case,**
that you may be acquitted. ²⁷ Your first father sinned,
and your mediators have transgressed against Me.*
*²⁸ Therefore I will **profane** the princes of the sanctuary; I
will give Jacob to the curse, and Israel to reproaches.
(Isaiah 43:22-28)(Emphasis mine)*

These are the issues God pointed out:

- You have not brought sheep for your burnt offerings;
- You have not honored Me with your sacrifices;

As a result:

- The Lord did not cause them to worship with incense
- They did not purchase the necessary frankincense as a fragrance to the LORD;
- Nor satisfied the LORD with the fragrance of offerings for their sins.
- **But** they burdened Me with their sins,
- They have wearied Me with their iniquities.

The children of Israel had messed up in a most severe way.
When we understand that we deal with three categories of sins,
then we can see that Israel had disobeyed in every one of them.

The categories are:

1. Transgressions - these are violations of written codes (laws). The Israelites had failed to properly offer sacrifices to the LORD, thus transgressing against him.

2. Sin - to disobey the will of God. It is to go against what you know in your heart is pleasing to God;

3. Iniquity - the propensity to do a particular kind of sin.

We actually see a progression of these three categories. The willful violation of the code of conduct (expressed in the Pentateuch (Genesis - Deuteronomy) leads to a willingness to violate the desire of God in the heart (see v. 24). This repetitive transgression and sin create a bend toward certain sins (i.e. alcoholism, adultery, cheating, stealing, etc.). Israel had fallen into this trap. Therefore the LORD invited them to come to the Court of Heaven and plead their case.

[25] *"I, even I, am He who **blots out your transgressions** for My own sake; and I will **not remember your sins.** [26] **Put Me in remembrance**; let us **contend** together; **state your case, that you may be acquitted.** [27] Your first father sinned, and your mediators have transgressed against Me. [28] Therefore I will **profane** the princes of the sanctuary; I will give Jacob to the curse, and Israel to reproaches. (Isaiah 43:25-28) (Emphasis mine)*

'He blots out your transgressions.' The commentator Albert Barnes describes this:

This metaphor is taken from the custom of keeping accounts, where, when a debt is paid, the charge is blotted or canceled. Thus God says he blotted out the sins of the Jews. He canceled them. He forgave them. Of course, when forgiven, punishment could not be exacted, and he would treat them as pardoned; that is, as his friends.[45]

Because the sins were blotted out, God no longer remembers them. At this point, the LORD invites Isaiah to come forward. The picture is of a courtroom scenario. The defendant comes into the Court with his/her attorney to contend with the prosecution. He is instructed to state *'your case so that you may be acquitted.'*

When it comes to the Courts of Heaven, we have a distinct advantage. We have a just judge who happens to be our Heavenly Father. He wants us to be victorious in court. He wants us to be acquitted. However, we have to come before Him as the Just Judge so He can.

He even helps out by explaining the problem:

[27] *Your first father sinned, and your mediators have transgressed against Me.* [28] *Therefore I will* **profane** *the princes of the sanctuary; I will give Jacob to the curse, and Israel to reproaches. (Isaiah 43:25-28)(Emphasis mine)*

Iniquity is the issue he is addressing here. In verse 24 He told us, *'You have* **wearied Me with your iniquities**.*' The things Isaiah had to do were to deal with two primary issues:

---

[45] Albert Barnes Notes on the Bible. (Isaiah 43:25). http://biblehub.com/commentaries/barnes/isaiah/43.htm. Access 8/30/2016.

The first one, *'Your first fathers sinned'* - The term 'first' means just that. Our father from the beginning sinned, and it created conditions that were impacting Isaiah's life. Although Isaiah was not responsible for Adam's sin, he was certainly affected by it. It is the same with us. I am not accountable for my great-great-great-grandfather's sins. Yet some of the things he did created consequences.

Science has proven that certain conditions can be passed down from generation to generation.

You're not an equal product of both parents' genes. Genomic imprinting, a process whereby only one gene copy is expressed, not only exists but, combined with mutations, may lead to disease.[46]

Other conditions have been found to be inherited in our DNA as well. Our DNA is the sum total of our ancestry, their experiences, the impact of their environment, their fears, as well as their physical and mental strengths or weaknesses.

Physically I inherited a propensity that caused a birth defect in my feet. Ancestrally, my great-grandfather was born with the same condition. He had a cousin with the same condition. I don't know how far back the situation went in my lineage. Neither he nor I sinned to invoke this inherited condition. We do not know who did. However, his life was impacted by it and so was mine.

---

[46] Lobo, I. (2008) Genomic Imprinting and Patterns of Disease Inheritance. Nature Education 1(1):66

Remember the man who was born blind who was healed by Jesus? The disciples asked Jesus, 'Did this man sin, or his parents?' It is ludicrous to think that the man sinned while in his mother's womb, and it would have resulted in his blindness. Jesus corrects their thinking concerning this. However, the point does remain that sin has consequences.

Certain fears can be inherited through the generations, a provocative study of mice reports. The authors suggest that a similar phenomenon could influence anxiety and addiction in humans.[47]

The same effect was found in descendants of Holocaust survivors. Researchers have also discovered that humans have an innate fear of snakes and their response to snakes is heightened in comparison to fears of other creatures. Could that be a part of the enmity God spoke to Eve about in the Garden of Eden?

We must be willing to repent on behalf of the conditions our forefathers invoked as a result of their sin. The adversary looks at your life to see if he can disqualify you from getting what God has promised. If he finds nothing he can use against you personally, the enemy will start climbing up the family tree to find something by which he can disqualify you.

You may say to yourself, "Well, I'll never be qualified then!" Not so. My friends, Jackie and Dan Hanselman have a book entitled "Silencing the Accuser: Restoration of Your

---

[47] Ewen Callaway, "Fearful Memories Haunt Mouse Descendants" Nature Publishing Group, December 1, 2013.

Birthright." This book contains a series of prayers covering all kinds of situations and conditions. It has been used quite effectively to bring about the cleansing of the bloodlines and healing of many things—physical as well as mental and emotional. We often work together as our ministries mesh quite well. You can find out more about this at www.silencingtheaccuser.com.

The second arena Isaiah had to deal with was found in verse 27:

...and your mediators have transgressed against Me.

The King James Version uses the term 'teachers.' The LORD was expressing to Isaiah that the spiritual leadership in his life was part of the problem. They had sinned against the LORD and had not taught the people properly. Our proper spiritual alignment is a critical aspect of our successful walk with God. Some are in leadership who cannot take you where you need to go. Some have disqualified themselves. Some we have followed for the wrong reasons and not out of instruction from Holy Spirit. That places you in a bad spot, and it puts those leaders in a bad spot. You, are in a bad spot because you are out of alignment with the will of God concerning your spiritual leadership. Your leaders are in a bad spot because they are overseeing someone not assigned to them. You are actually creating a vulnerability for them. If you are assigned to a ministry, and you refuse to obey, or you leave prematurely, you create exploitable areas. You create areas of vulnerability in your life and in the life of the ministry you are involved in (assuming you are involved in a ministry), and you are also creating a void in the ministry you should be part of. We need to be properly aligned with the leadership God has for us. They have something to impart into our lives, and we can miss that impartation by being in the wrong place.

The LORD points out to Isaiah the result of these problems:

²⁸ Therefore I will profane the princes of the sanctuary; I will give Jacob to the curse, and Israel to reproaches. (Isaiah 43:28)

The princes of the sanctuary refer to those who governed the affairs of the presence of God -- spiritual leaders. By being profaned, they become ordinary people...no longer set apart for holy service.

Jacob was given to the curse - or reproach. Jacob was a reference to the natural leaders among them, those responsible for the welfare of the people.

Israel was given over to reproaches. They lost their reputation and their favor before God.

We must deal with the things that hinder us from receiving all God has in mind for us. Isaiah was placed in the position to repent for the sins of his forefathers and his spiritual leaders. God desired restoration for His people, but repentance was required. Often, we want God to do things for us, but want nothing to do with repentance. Repentance positions you to receive from God.

God's desire to bless His people is detailed in Isaiah 44 where he will restore and help. That is His heart. He just asks that we be willing to step in and repent on behalf of ourselves and others so His blessings can be released in fuller measure.

CHAPTER 12:

THE PARTIES IN THE COURTROOM

*O*n a typical courtroom, you will find several people. You have the judge, the prosecuting attorney, the defense attorney (in our case, Jesus in Heaven and Holy Spirit on earth); the defendant, the accusers, witnesses, recorders, bailiffs, and sometimes others. Sometimes lawyers will bring in experts to advise them on individual components of the trial. We have access to the Seven Spirits of God.

THE JUDGE

Jehovah God is our judge in the Mercy Court.

Shall not the Judge of all the earth do right?" (Genesis 18:25)

David cried out,

Vindicate (judge) me, O God, and plead my cause against an ungodly nation; Oh, deliver me from the deceitful and unjust man! (Psalm 43:1) (Emphasis mine)

And again,

Vindicate (judge) me, O LORD my God, according to Your righteousness; and let them not rejoice over me. (Psalm 35:24) (Emphasis mine)

THE PROSECUTING ATTORNEY

Satan, our opponent, will typically fill this role as he is the one in charge of bringing accusations. In Zechariah 3 we find him coming to challenge Joshua the High Priest. We mentioned this story earlier. An accuser is a legal opponent. 1 Peter 5:8 refers to our adversary as the devil.

THE DEFENSE ATTORNEY

In John 14:16-17 we read:

*[16]I-am seeking from my Father to give you **another defense attorney** that will be with you forever. [17]The Spirit-wind has the truth. (ARTB) (Emphasis mine)*

And again:

*[26]The **defense attorney is the holy Spirit-wind** that my Father is dispatching in my name. He will teach you everything, and he will recall for you what all I said to you. (John 14:26 ARTB) (Emphasis mine)*

Typical translations render the word comforter, while others use the word 'advocate.' The term advocate has legal meaning, however 'comforter' implies to us that he is like a warm blanket. Holy Spirit is far more than that. An implication also exists that Jesus, while on earth was our defense attorney. Now that he is in the presence of the Father, he serves in that role. Other Scriptures point him out as our Mediator[48].

THE DEFENDANT

That would be us, or the person(s) we are bringing before the court. We have the ability to bring others before the Court of Heaven. Sometimes individuals in need do not have the ability, or knowledge to go into the Courts of Heaven and need someone to work on their behalf, like the parents of the young lady in the story related earlier. It is in this role as intercessors (go-betweens) that much freedom can be brought into people's lives. We have seen remarkable results as we have used the 'secret weapon' of the Courts of Heaven to deal with things impacting others' lives.

THE ACCUSERS

Sometimes we can call in others who are making the accusations (their spirits can go where their bodies may not want to go). Sometimes the accusations are being voiced by specific demonic entities. They can be called into court in these situations.

WITNESSES

---

[48] 1 Timothy 2:5; Hebrews 8:6; 9:15; 12:24.

In most courts you have witnesses appear who can give pertinent testimony to the matters at hand. In the Courts of Heaven, you have a similar scenario. The Bible refers to a great cloud of witnesses[49]. These witnesses are part of the church. The Aramaic word for witness is *ed* from which the word *edah* is derived. *Edah* is an assemblage (or company) of witnesses. It is the Aramaic word for 'church.' The Greek word for church is 'ecclesia' meaning an assembly or gathering. The writer of Hebrews is reminding us that we are surrounded by a vast assembly of witnesses—those who testify. We cannot reference the word 'cloud' to find out more as that is the only time in the New Testament it was used. However, in the literature of the period, the phrase was often used to designate a great multitude.

Paul pointed out to us that the church is comprised of those believers living on the earth, and those believers who have gone on before us. He considers us one body. He does not consider those who have gone on before as being dead or non-existent. They simply have a different address, and it is not the local cemetery.

Now, therefore, you are no longer strangers and foreigners, but fellow citizens with the saints and members of the household of God... (Ephesians 2:19)

---

[49] Hebrews 12:1 Therefore we also, since we are surrounded by so great a cloud of witnesses, let us lay aside every weight, and the sin which so easily ensnares us, and let us run with endurance the race that is set before us....

We are fellow citizens with the saints. We are all members of God's household. We are family. Paul noted that 'to be absent from the body... was to be... present with the Lord.' (2 Corinthians 5:8)

The fact that we, and these witnesses, are citizens of Heaven is one of the ways we know we have a right to be functioning in the Courts of Heaven.

Remember too, that the more credible the witness, the greater the impact of their testimony. I have been aware of witnesses who have been present in the Courts of Heaven. On one occasion I heard the testimony of one witness saying, "Yes Your Honor, they did that for me while I was upon the earth!" [Note, we are not talking about necromancy (consulting the dead). These individuals are not dead as far as God is concerned. They are very much alive!]

RECORDERS

These beings (angelic in the Mercy Court) record the happenings within the court, just as most court systems have someone who records the proceedings we see the same pattern in the Courts of Heaven. They create records of the actions in the court and the decisions of the court.

BAILIFFS

In natural courts, these are typically deputies who serve the court as protectors. In the Courts of Heaven, we find angels fulfilling these roles.

THE SEVEN SPIRITS OF GOD

These are our experts in the Courts of Heaven. I will not go into a lengthy discussion about them or their role. I will only point out who the seven spirits of God are. They are not the Holy Spirit, they are separate entities. In Revelation 1:4 we find that they are before the throne. In Isaiah 11:2 we find:

The Spirit of the LORD shall rest upon Him, The Spirit of wisdom and understanding, The Spirit of counsel and might, The Spirit of knowledge and of the fear of the LORD. (Isaiah 11:2)

Seven entities are listed:

1) Spirit of the LORD
2) Spirit of wisdom
3) Spirit of understanding
4) Spirit of counsel
5) Spirit of might
6) Spirit of knowledge
7) Spirit of the fear of the LORD

Each of these has contributions that can be invaluable to us as we access the Courts of Heaven. They know the operations of the Courts and know what to do in every situation. We need to learn to avail ourselves of their wisdom. We will be richer for it.

In a court, you need each of these attributes working for you. We want the Spirit of the Lord present. When you need wisdom, consult the Spirit of Wisdom. When you need understanding, ask the spirit of understanding. When you need counsel, ask him. Do the same with might, knowledge, and the fear of the Lord.

These provide expert knowledge about every situation. We need to avail ourselves of them, not merely when going into a courtroom of Heaven.

CHAPTER 13:

THE PROTOCOL

OF THE MERCY COURT

*W*hen teaching the Mercy Court Seminar, I teach extensively on protocol. Merriam-Webster's Dictionary defines protocol as:

a system of rules that explain the correct conduct and procedures to be followed in formal situations[50]

Protocols are the ways we are to conduct ourselves. In Matthew 5 Jesus taught extensively on the protocol for various actions.

BRINGING A GIFT

---

[50] "Definition of Protocol." *Definition of Protocol.* Merriam-Webster, n.d. Web. 31 Aug. 2016. <http://www.merriam-webster.com/dictionary/protocol>.

Beginning at verse 23:

Therefore if you bring your gift to the altar, and there remember that your brother has something against you, ²⁴ leave your gift there before the altar, and go your way. First, be reconciled to your brother, and then come and offer your gift. (Matthew 5:23-24)

- Action: Bringing a gift to the altar.
- Protocol: Reflect to see if your brother has something against you. If so, go and be reconciled to your brother and then bring the gift.

Going to Court

²⁵ Agree with your adversary quickly, while you are on the way with him, lest your adversary delivers you to the judge, the judge hand you over to the officer, and you be thrown into prison. ²⁶ Assuredly, I say to you, you will by no means get out of there till you have paid the last penny. (Matthew 5:25-26)

- Action: Going to court
- Protocol: Agree with your adversary quickly.
- Result: If you don't follow the instruction, you may be thrown into prison.

Jesus goes on to discuss anger, lust, divorce, oaths, retaliation, and loving your enemies. In Matthew 6, the same discourse is continuing where he explains the protocol for charitable deeds, prayer, and fasting.

Concerning charitable acts, he instructs us to not let everyone know what you are doing. With the subject of prayer he modeled the Son to Father protocol of prayer. Finally, he discusses fasting discreetly. Each of the protocols for these actions was designed to keep the focus off of the individual and on to the proper response before God.

COURTROOM PROTOCOL

Protocols are also involved in the way we are to conduct ourselves in the courtroom. In a natural court, you dress a certain way. In the spirit, we come in the robes of righteousness. You don't come in dressed for war. Rather, you dress for the courtroom.

In a natural court, you would be required to check your weapons at the door. You speak respectfully to the Judge. Although He is our Father, he is still the Judge of the Universe.

When I look at the function of the different positions within the Mercy Court several things stand out:

1) Only one judge is present. We don't have multiple judges in this court. You are not the judge, nor are you the jury. You certainly are not the executioner.
2) The Judge does not need your help to do His job. Let Him do the judging while you do the repenting.
3) If you are the defendant, act like the defendant. Speak respectfully and as necessary.
4) Always be open to repent should Holy Spirit indicate to you that something needs to be dealt with.

5) Come in with humility of heart. A haughty spirit will not help you in this Court.
6) Present your case respectably. Do your homework before you enter the courtroom. Do your best. Most likely you will not know everything you would like to know before going into the courtroom. Go in exercising your faith and expecting God to render a verdict on your behalf or on behalf of the one(s) you are going to court for.

CHAPTER 14:

THE MERCY COURT QUICKGUIDE

*H*aving taught dozens of seminars on the Mercy Court, it was apparent from the very beginning that people be able to implement what I was teaching. Over the course of time, I have refined this QuickGuide for the purpose of doing just that. I have templates available in Word.docx format that can be downloaded so you can "fill in the blank," so to speak. It has never been my intent that these Quickguides become "mechanical." When using them, we must be flexible and listen to the Father, Jesus, Holy Spirit and the Seven Spirits of God, as well as any others who may be permitted to speak.

As you follow along with this QuickGuide, you will get a feel for the typical procedure. I, as well as others, have used this QuickGuide hundreds of times and have seen lives changed through this paradigm of prayer.

While going through the QuickGuide, you may realize that you need more information. All you have to do is ask the court for a recess. It is like the Pause button on your DVD player. It pauses everything until you are able to return to the case. At which point, you will just resume the case. The fact that we are able to come back to the court was something the widow woman in Luke 18 understood. She was intent on returning as often as necessary. Using the pause in the Mercy Court seems to suspend whatever is going on. The enemy is restricted from doing further damage and must wait until the Court is back in session.

Let me reiterate. The QuickGuide is to help you along. It is not to become a formal, mechanical approach to dealing with accusations. If your heart is not right when you go into the Mercy Court, do not expect to have positive results. Our Father, the Just Judge, wants to see lives restored. He has unveiled this new tool so we can become more efficient in working with Him to bring people to freedom.

MERCY COURT QUICKGUIDE

You or the party for whom you are going to Court is the Defendant.

Pray along these lines:

Father God, our Just Judge, I ask to enter the Courts of Heaven today, not on my own account but through the blood of Jesus. I request that I be seen only in His Righteousness in this Court today.

I ask that Jesus Christ opens all books on my behalf, from Heaven and Hell during this court session, that all Records may be reviewed and judged, and that the Court rulings may be manifested on earth, according to Father God.

I address this Court in the blood of Jesus and in the Righteousness of Jesus. I ask through Jesus, my Advocate, that all Court parties be present including the accuser of the brethren and his dark forces, the great cloud of witnesses that has testimony on my behalf, the angelic hosts working for the Just Judge to enact His judgments, and the Seven Spirits of God.

PRESENTATION OF ACCUSATIONS:

Today, I bring to Your Honor, through my Mediator, Jesus Christ, the following list of charges made against ____(me/defendant)____ by myself, others, and the workers of darkness.

Present each accusation individually if possible.

Your Honor, I present the accusation that "_____." According to Matthew 5:25, I agree with my adversary, and I confess this as sin. I repent of this sin and ask that the blood of Jesus be applied to this sin and all the ramifications of it, in Jesus' name.

I ask forgiveness for any action or reaction on my part that caused this accusation to be made by (____me, others____), and I ask that it and all ramifications of it be cleansed by the blood of Jesus.

On the basis of John 20:23, I choose to forgive _(name of parties making the accusation)_ for their judgments against me, and I ask Our Father, the Just Judge, to forgive them.

I choose to forgive (the Defendant if not yourself) of their sin in this matter and ask you to forgive it as well, Your Honor.

Repeat this process for each accusation.

Your Honor, I wish to repent for those things I have spoken against __(me/the Defendant)_ and ask your forgiveness of these words spoken, in Jesus' name. I ask that the blood of Jesus is applied to this sin and that it would be entirely erased from existence.

CALLING OF WITNESSES:

Your Honor, we would request that those who have testimony in _(my/the Defendants')_ behalf, be called forward at this time.

At this point, have the seers with you to begin to listen and see who has presented themselves and have them give their testimony. At this time, the Great Cloud of Witnesses may step up and provide further support of your faith in Jesus and walk with God. The Holy Spirit may even call forth a saint who is interceding on your behalf.

SUBMISSION OF TESTIMONY:

Your Honor, I now submit through the blood of Jesus this testimony of my life in Christ.

Present evidence of your journey of faith.

Your Honor, at this time I would like to present the following promises from the Word of God concerning this Defendant:

Recite particular pertinent promises from the Word of God at this time.

Further, Your Honor, I would also like to present the following as testimony in _(the Defendants')_ behalf.

Recite/read prophetic words given concerning the Defendant.

CLOSING STATEMENT:

Your Honor, we would request of the court the following:

In the closing statement provide your suggested recourse if there has been an injustice made against you (financial, relationship, etc. to be restored, perpetrators to be saved, etc.).

I also ask the Courts regarding all accusations made against (the Defendant) by the accuser of the brethren to be stricken/purged from all records (Heaven and Hell, and with all reference to these accusations) that I have petitioned today in the blood of Jesus.

After the judge has made a ruling on the case, He will give a court decision. The other side (accuser of the brethren) must be properly served notice of the finding of the Judge. The court deputies, the angelic host, will administer all records, and implement the courts' rulings. Records will be closed after being purged of accusations with the blood of Jesus covering your sin. The court is adjourned. Celebrate!

Take Communion! Celebrating Communion is a wonderful way to seal your courtroom work. It calls us to remembrance of the covenant made with us through Jesus.

Chapter 15:

In Conclusion

As you exercise your faith and begin operating in the Courts of Heaven, you will find the promise of the Lord to respond speedily coming to pass in your life.

By engaging the Courts of Heaven you have the opportunity to change your life, lives within your family, your church, city, state, and even your nation. Recent major events have been impacted due to actions of believers in the Courts of Heaven.

Believers across the globe are awakening to the potential within this paradigm of prayer. Lives are being changed. Cities are being changed. Even the political landscape is being affected by courtroom prayer. As we become more well-versed in the operations of this court, we will see the command of Jesus to disciple nations coming to fulfillment. May we indeed, disciple the nations!

APPENDIX

As citizens of Heaven, we have far more rights and privileges than we have exercised. As you engage the courts, you will see victories on a massive scale in your life. A couple of the tools available to us are the Request for Continuance, and the Cease and Desist Order. Other legal maneuvers exist, but these are the most used (in my experience).

REQUEST FOR CONTINUANCE

Receiving a Fair Trial is Your Right as a Citizen of Heaven

You just found out that you have to go to court! What do you do? You have not had time to prepare, and you have not had a chance to sit down with your attorney (in our case Jesus) and discuss the best way to proceed. Your solution: Seek a "Request for Continuance"!

In our natural court system the option of a "Request for Continuance" exists to ensure a fair trial. Now that you understand that such a place as the "Court of Heaven" exists, you can now begin to be much wiser in your response to Satan's attacks and schemes. Just as you would in a natural court, you can obtain a "Request for Continuance" in a couple of ways:

(1) Petition the Clerk of Court (in our case Holy Spirit for a continuance),

(2) Go before the Judge (God, our Father) and request a continuance. Note before him that you need ample time to prepare for this trial and time to consult with your attorney. Just as in the natural, our Judge, wants us to experience a "fair trial" and will grant this request. A continuance does not put off a trial indefinitely. Generally, it can be put off for a few days or weeks so request a continuance for at least four (4) weeks. This should give you ample time to get yourself prepared for trial.

Also, request a "Cease and Desist Order" so that all current activity against you about the trial at hand is stayed. Following is a template dealing with a Cease & Desist in relation to "Defamation of Character." Other types of Cease & Desist letters can be issued as well.

The Bible says, "You have not because you ask not" it really means it. Now that we know about these things, though, we can begin to "ask and receive that (our) joy may be full.

The procedure for requesting a continuance is simple:

1) Ask to enter the Court of Heaven
2) Come before the judge and request the continuance:
   a. "Your honor, I am requesting a continuance on _____ (the matter at hand) so that I might better prepare my case. I would request at least _____ (name the time frame) in order to prepare to bring this case before this court.

3) Thank the Court: Thank you, your Honor.

It is that simple. I have never known a request of this sort to be denied. As I mentioned, however, it is not a means of indefinitely putting off a case. You must deal with it in a reasonable fashion, just as you would in a natural court system.

If you are given any instructions while in the court, make sure you follow those instructions.

CEASE & DESIST ORDER

Knowing what you can do is vital!

We have all experienced harassment and infringement of our rights by the enemy, demons, and sometimes people. However, we don't have to put up with everything that comes our way. As we learn to operate in the Courts of Heaven we see that many of the principles utilized in the natural court system can be applied to the Court of Heaven. After all, they got their ideas from God!

A Cease & Desist Order is one of those concepts. Since Satan is a legalist, we have to be just as exacting as he is. In the natural arena, Cease & Desist letters can be issued by an individual or by attorneys acting on behalf of their clients. Cease & Desist Orders can be issued for a variety of reasons, not limited to, but including:

- Defamation, Slander, and Libel
- Trademark Infringement
- Copyright Infringement
- Patent Infringement
- Harassment
- Debt Collection
- Breach of Contract

You can easily see how many (if not all) of these situations could apply to us. To utilize a Cease & Desist Order, you can simply go before the Court of Heaven and request a Cease & Desist Order be issued due to the harassment/defamation/

slander, etc. (or whatever is occurring) that you are experiencing. It matters not whether it is demonic in nature or coming through a person because ultimately it is a spiritual battle we are engaged in. Let us learn to fight via the Courts of Heaven.

Much like the request for a continuance, it is a similar process. God, our Father, is willing to aid us and is ready to dispatch angels to assist us in these issues. As part of your request for a Cease & Desist, also ask that angels be sent to enforce the order. My final word to you:

Enjoy your victorious position!

BIBLIOGRAPHY

Barnes, Albert. Isaiah 43 Barnes Notes. n.d. 30 August 2016 <http://biblehub.com/commentaries/barnes/isaiah/43.htm>.

Brenton, Sir Lancelot Charles Lee. Translation of the Greek Septuagint into English. Public Domain, n.d.

Callaway, Ewen. "Fearful Memories Haunt Mouse Descendants." 1 December 2013. Nature News. 30 August 2016 <http://www.nature.com/news/fearful-memories-haunt-mouse-descendants-1.14272>.

Clarke, Adam. The Adam Clarke Commentary. 1832, Public Domain.

Crossway. ESV® Bible (The Holy Bible, English Standard Version®). Nashville: Good News Publishers, 2001.

Foundation, The Lockman. The Amplified Bible. Grand Rapids: Zondervan, 1958.

Horner, Dr. Ron M. Overcoming Verdicts from the Courts of Hell. Albemarle: LifeSpring Publishing, 2016.

Lobo, Ingrid I., Ph.D. "Genomic Imprinting and Patterns of Disease Inheritance." 2008. Nature Education. 30 August 2016 <http://www.nature.com/scitable/topicpage/genomic-imprinting-and-patterns-of-disease-inheritance-899>.

Merriam-Webster.com. http://www.merriam-webster.com/dictionary/protocol. n.d. 31 August 2016 <http://www.merriam-webster.com/dictionary/protocol>.

Moffat, James. James Moffat Translation of the New Testament. Chicago: The University of Chicago Press, 1926.

Murdock, James. James Murdock New Testament. 1851, Public Domain.

Strong, James. The New Strong's Expanded Exhaustive Concordance of the Bible. Nashville: Thomas-Nelson, 2010.

Theopedia.com. Theopedia. n.d. 3 August 2016 <http://www.theopedia.com/prooftexting>.

Thomas Nelson. New King James Version. Nashville: Thomas Nelson Publishers, 1982.

DESCRIPTION

*I*n Luke 18 Jesus subtly introduces a third paradigm of prayer. The courtroom model has gone overlooked throughout church history. Only in the last few years has this truth been uncovered with amazing results. Prayers that have long gone unanswered are being answered in a matter of days or even hours. Situations from which no hope seemed available are turning around.

This truth is for every believer, but it will also help thrust intercession efforts into new levels of breakthrough. Once every legal obstacle hindering the answer to your prayers is removed, the answers will come. As we learn to engage the Courts of Heaven, lives will change...your life will change. You will experience answered prayer on a level you may have not thought possible.

Grasp these truths and begin to engage the Courts of Heaven. The court is now in session....all rise!

ABOUT THE AUTHOR

*D*r. Ron Horner is an apostolic teacher specializing in Overturning Verdicts from the Courts of Hell, Local Church Government, Freedom from Captivity, and the subject of this book -- The Court System of Heaven. He is married and the father of three daughters (two of whom are married), and grandfather to Ike. He resides in central North Carolina with his wife, Adina and youngest daughter, Darian.

RECOMMENDED RESOURCES

vercoming Verdicts from the Courts of Hell
by Dr. Ron M. Horner
Paperback (140 pages): $14.99
Kindle Edition or eBook Edition: $7.99

Have you found yourself struggling with situations or mindsets from which you could find no relief? We have not yet awakened to the fact that way may have been facing a false judgment arising out of the Courts of Hell. Jesus promised us in Matthew 16:18 that the Gates of Hell would not prevail against the church, but that promise was predicated on our using the keys effectively--the keys of binding and loosing! This is not your typical "binding and loosing" book -- it explores a whole different dimension and unveils what you are dealing with and how to successfully overcome these false judgments affecting our lives. You need this book NOW!

Available at www.overcomingverdicts.com

*S*ilencing the Accuser
Restoration of Your Spiritual Birthright
(Third Edition)
by Jacquelin & Daniel Hanselman
Paperback: $19.95
Kindle Edition or eBook Edition: $9.99

The Body of Christ is being destroyed by lack of knowledge, wisdom, and understanding of the captivity of individuals, families, cities, and even nations caused by generational and personal accusations. The reality of the goodness of God is challenged by the stark contrast between the covenantal blessings promised in the Word of God and the struggles in one's life.

In this book, the Hanselman's uncover the source of these hindrances with practical teachings and prayers that will help you be cleared of the charges against you and your family in the Court of Heaven. Allow the Just Judge to declare you innocent by the Blood of the Lamb as you agree with your accuser in generational and personal repentance. Now is the time to begin the process of dismantling the accusations of the enemy! Families, regions, and nations can be set free by the application of these prayers. It is time for the destiny of the Body of Christ to be released for the great end time harvest.

Available at www.silencingtheaccuser.com

Made in the USA
San Bernardino, CA
30 April 2017